Better Days

Kerry R. Jeffrey

A journal based book of sorts. From darkness to light, there's always better days.

Dedication

Needless to say that this part of the book was the last thing I wrote of this book. It was one of the truly hardest dedications I had to make. It shouldn't have but it was truly hard for me to put these words down at this time.

This dedication is the one I have wanted to write for some time. It wasn't easy for me to write this one because it is unlike other dedications that I have of my other books. This one took some deep soul searching. I really just wanted to include everyone that has brought me here. To dedicate something for the ones who know my heart. They are the ones that got me to this point. They got me to where I could find it in me to write an in-depth autographical yet kind of self-help book.

To all my parents: Without them I wouldn't be here. Thanks for your support, your love and understanding of me, someone so different, so caring, and so unwavering in my efforts to make others happy.

To my brothers and sister: With siblings as friends, one can never fall. Thanks for seeing me as an older brother, even though I never seem to act as one. Thanks for letting me be the clown when all I tried to hide was hurt. Thanks for taking care of me, sometimes more than you know.

To my friends (my other family): If you hadn't put me in a place to where I could grow then we wouldn't be here.

To my wonderful friend Amy Baird: I have complete gratitude for your sweet heart and the place you have held in mine. I can never thank God enough for you. Thanks for the hugs and the smiles.

To my daughter Katie, my one and only: I am proud to show you how a father like me can show you a love I never thought I would have...an undying one. Your happiness is always more important than mine.

Table of Contents

10. Teach me how to speak

Teach me how to share

11. I told dirty jokes

until you smiled

12. ...you're already the

voice inside my head

13. Why does love always

feel like a battlefield

14. It's not a question

but a lesson learned in time

15. I'll keep your

memory vague

16. No one sings

like you anymore

17. Take me as I come

because I can't stay long

18. Just a chance that maybe

we'll find better days

19. You can go

You can start all over again

20. Love will keep

us alive

21. Standing all alone

against the world outside

22. You're the meaning in my life

You're the inspiration

23. And All Of My Flaws

Are Laid Out One By One

24. Stuck in the middle with you

25. But if it's love you're looking for,

then I can give a little more

26. We'll burn that bridge

when we get there

27. The closer you get

the harder I fall

28. Now don't you understand

that I'm never changing who I am

29. The hook brings you back
on that you can rely

30. I never dreamed I'd

love somebody like you

Introduction

I started this book when I was sixteen years old. Needless to say it took me awhile to finally finish it (At the age of thirty to be exact). Originally, I wrote it as two books. It has a lot in it. I do realize that it's probably not close to being the best in the world but it is my own. A great bit of time went into it and it has good meaning. It started out as a journal that I wrote my thoughts down in, but now it is so much more. It all stems from being heartbroken at a young age. I did try to write this more like a book than a journal. Although, I did try to preserve some of what the original journal had in it. There was no sense in rewriting it. I hope it's one of a kind. I wanted it to be a little different. Well, taking for granted, I haven't read that many books in my life either.

There are a couple of reasons why this turned from a journal into a book. I was tired of holding it in. Because, as a male at sixteen, I was exhausted in the way of trying to explain myself and my actions. I had felt that the world did not care to know why I spent so much time in isolation away from others. Why I was lost sometimes. Why I felt so heartbroken and incomplete. I tried to reach out from the inside and often felt that no one tried to reach back. These words was good therapy for me. I just needed to see them formed on paper. I wanted to show the world that people like me were here; I existed. I was a tender-hearted, compassionate male that didn't know how to express it. I wanted to share how depression along with the fight to love others and learning to love life is a battle. A battle a lot of us face day after day.

I believe there is really no cure for depression. A lot of people think that everything can be cured by medicine, self help clinics, therapy, or faith.

In which, I believe a lot of people have been helped through these methods. I don't judge. I wanted to take another path. I chose to write and to pursue the tenderness I so thrived for.

This is my autobiography, self-help book that I always needed.

This book will at times seem to read a little choppy... like a journal. It was purposely done so to convey thoughts and emotions. This is a book of love, heartache, depression, and realizations. It shares a dedication of life, love, art, people, music, and most of all, a strength in compassion.

You'll notice throughout this book the chapters are named by referencing music song titles and lyrics of songs. I believe songs often speak of what the heart can't tell. The more you read the more you'll understand. Music relates to us on so many levels. I listen to music that says and means things to me. Music is the poetry of the vibrant heart.

Thanks for reading.

Chapter One

Somewhere in this darkness
there's a light that I can't find

To me, life presented itself as if it was one big black tunnel! I feel I had to compare it to something and this is what came about. I say this for the simple fact that in my mind it makes sense. It was a black tunnel because like one, I felt like there was nothing around me. It seemed that no one understood what I could put myself through. I had all these emotions that I wanted to express but I couldn't. I still don't understand completely why I thought this way.

My black tunnel had these light spots that would show up on occasion. I guess they were there to light the path at times so I wouldn't get too lost. Later, these lights, these spots turned into the missing portions of emotion that I thought was missing. Love was one of the major portions. I always sought the love that I thought wasn't there. So, when one of the spots appeared, I would try to hold on as long as possible. Hanging on too tight or too long would smother the lights and make them disappear. With these disappearances, I felt that I was all the more lost.

My family was never quite a big part of my tunnel. They existed outside the tunnel. I think that if they were I would've had more problems than I did. My father and mother tried there best to keep me protected and sheltered. I don't know why it was but I thought my childhood was very lonely. Although, I had my brother and sister there to keep me company, the memories still remain that I felt lonely. We had a simple childhood. We lived in the woods outside of town and really didn't see many people that lived around us. We preoccupied our time with climbing trees, building club houses out of scrap wood, playing in the creek, and every once in a while, the occasional horse apple fight. Our cousins lived right up the hill, but we didn't see them as much as we liked either. I, along with my siblings, spent a lot of time at home with our thoughts because we had hardly any money to go anywhere. Dad worked for us while Momma stayed home to take care of us three. We were taught to create our own brand of happiness.

Unfortunately, Mom and Dad separated when I was eleven. I'm not going to say that this is the start of all the controversy, because I don't believe it myself. Maybe, in the background, it played a tiny part.

My idea of love wasn't there in the beginning. That's why I spent most of my young and some of my adult life trying to pursue the love that I thought was nothing more than a spot of light. I always wanted someone to love me back. (A light that wouldn't disappear.)

I believe that one of the things in life that cannot be totally understood is love itself. I know that there are many types of it. One type is the one you already have. The one you're born with. I refer to it as pure love. This is the one that I believe calms you as a child to hear your mother's voice when you're hurt.

I heard someone try to define love (It's probably a quote by someone famous or just something he had heard from a movie) and I have stuck with that definition for some time now. He said that it is neither past nor future but the present. Live for it, for all too soon it will slip away.

The other love is true love, which a lot more people believe in than they will admit to. They say that this is the greatest love of all. It possibly is, if you have it. Truly, this being totally different from its counterpart. It's different because it has to be achieved. Somehow you know it's going to last. You undoubtedly know that this person is a part of you. You grow cold and isolated when you are apart, but warm up with the smallest piece of a telephone call. Without them, you can't breathe and with them, you're left breathless. Love is the miracle that makes the world simple. Sometimes, the miracle is simply falling in love.

No matter what your opinion is on love, you have to admit that the greatest love of all is the one you fought for and won!

Chapter Two

It's happened once again

I'll turn to a friend

School was a somewhat happy medium in my life. I looked towards going there. It was time away from my room. Sure the work was hard at times, but I did it. Some teachers made studying fun; others were just boring. Third grade was the turn around year and I say this because everything starts to matter then.

I can honestly say that I had all female friends. Sadly, I was bullied in school for that reason. It was always said that a guy couldn't stay friends with a female long because it comes to a time where he likes her for more than one. So, as time grew on, my innocent friendships with the other party grew to crushes. I didn't want to hang out with the guys. The stuff that interested the other guys didn't interest me in the slightest. All I truly wanted to do was know the girls. Talk of cars, stereos, and fighting didn't interest me. I wanted to hang with the girls because they had more to say and I could talk to them. (Weird, I know)

I'm soft hearted and I got hurt easily. (More times than not to say the least.) Girls can also be cruel at times, and I took most of what they said to heart. I just couldn't understand the difference between me and them. I never considered girls having cooties at that age. I was different and I guess that is why the girls let me hang around.

Some of my sadness started seeping in when my parent's divorce took place. I started going downhill and I didn't have a clue. I started to become a little clingy towards my friends and I guess they thought that was strange. So, they thought the more they pushed away, the more reliant I would become towards myself. I got my feelings hurt most of the time.

The problem was that my friends did not want to see me in a loving perspective. This was really upsetting because I wanted to love someone but no one wanted to love me. Tracy Montgomery was my first crush. Maria Morales was my second and the list goes on. My mom was a friend to Tracy's Mom and sometimes that created a problem. I thought that if Mom was a friend with Mrs. Montgomery, I would have a better chance at having Tracy as my girlfriend. As for Maria, she was a free spirit that I could not catch. I gave up quickly on the idea of us being together. I remember crying about that in fourth grade.

When I was eleven, I had my very first girlfriend and my very first heart break. Our family always knew each other but we didn't get to meet each other until later on. Her name was Kendra. She was this cute, curly headed, sweet yet funny little girl with the sweetest smile. We met on a playground when I cracked my mid-section on a wet bar that I was trying to balance on. That still hurts to think about. We lived in two different cities, so it was difficult to see each other. I used to beg my mom to go to town. To me, Kendra was everything wonderful about life.

I saw her as many times as I could and it lasted for a while. She taught me things that I never knew. I knew that I would love her forever. Later, she got back together with one of her old boyfriends and had her friend call me for her. Until this day, I remember that conversation.

Moving on...

"Affection Syndrome", is what I chose to call my emotional problems. It came from the feeling that I wanted someone to be there for me as a companion and finding out that they didn't want me. Depression was not a word in my terminology then, but I sure felt it.

Sometimes I wanted to be left alone, but I wanted someone there to listen. I wanted to be at peace with myself but everything in my life was so unstable. I started hiding my feelings from everyone, even my family. I covered it up well. I built the biggest wall I could and then a moat to go around it. I started to become a busybody.

I kept myself busy with poetry and art most of the time. The way I hid my feelings was to joke, laugh, and act like a crazy immature little kid. So, when I was really feeling down, the happier and hyper I acted. Every so often I would let it be known that something was bothering me but only when I thought I wasn't being a burden to anyone.

As for my crushes they only got worse, but no one knew. I kept them a secret. I figured if no one knew about them, I was less likely to get hurt. I remember I had a crush on this girl named Jennifer. I liked her for it seems forever. I could not figure out why she dated some of the guy's she did, but still the feelings remained. I eventually gave up on her as well (mostly because I couldn't see her actually liking me). Again, I blamed it on "the syndrome".

Although, I didn't like change, it eventually comes and gets us anyway. I was now thirteen and it was the middle of the summer when Dad set me, my brother, and my sister down for a talk. He told us that a friend of his was going to come and see us. Martha was her name and Dad had met her when he was younger and then again when he went to the Red Cross meetings in our town. So, it came down to that she was to be Dad's girlfriend and we were going to see more of her. After a while, Dad had found more work in East Texas and told us we were going to move. There was quite a bit more work for him there and that is where Martha's mom and dad lived. This now meant that we were going to experience a newer school and a newer life.

So, we moved right after I passed sixth grade. I had failed the grade the previous year and had to take it again. It wasn't that I wasn't smart enough to do so. It's just I didn't seem to care about a whole lot then. Seventh grade in a small town that was smaller than the one we left...Great! Of course, I'm being sarcastic.

Talk about being nervous. I think I talked to one person the whole day that wasn't a teacher. Although, there were a lot of attractive girls to possibly make friends with, maybe even go out with. I really wanted someone to be around if I needed to talk or felt lonely. And looking back, I went through several girlfriends. Even if I wanted to name a few, my idea of a lot wouldn't be as much as some. I rather tell you about the more important ones; ones that lasted for more than a week or two. Of course, I had more crushes than actual relationships. So, there was one I had my eye on but never chased after. The first day at school I met Rachel. She had jet black hair with the hint of brown, the hourglass figure, the deep brown eyes, and the soul of an angel. We were friends for the longest time. We sat together in history class and talked while we worked. I hung on every last word that came from those sweet lips. I loved to make her laugh. Her cheeks turned flush when she laughed too hard. I was totally enveloped by her. There are some people you never forget and she was top of the list. She was everything I wanted then but never had. I wanted to ask her out so many times before, but sadly fear took its toll and I was never brave enough to stand up to it. Instead, I tried to show her that I longed for her by doing things like drawing for her and being there as a listening ear. My moment of truth, that I never had, was in fact that I loved Rachel, but something told me that I could never tell her.

There were plenty more little crushes along the way but not really worth mentioning in the way of helping me in the least.

Then Mandy came along! She wasn't comparable to Rachel but she was cute. She was a brutally blunt speaking blonde and I loved it. I fell hard for this one. The crush lasted four years and even after high school I missed seeing her. I always drew on her hand for the simple pleasure of holding it. We talked about her boyfriend and more importantly why she should leave him. So, things changed and I lost touch with her after I graduated. I had a lot more interests but half of them will never know I even knew them.

Sadly, other half will see this book on a shelf and say in realization, "Hey, that reminds me of this guy I know...that I knew."

Chapter Three

I'm scared to death

I'm taking a chance; letting you inside

I think I should start out with a sort of middle and work with some flashbacks at this point. In my head and with the way it was written in the journal, it conveys better that way. Just to see the events that put me in the present. In 1998, I moved back to North Texas, back to where I had lived for the better part of my young life. This wasn't too much later after I got out of boot camp. Needless to say, we will cover this later. I promise.

Anyway, I landed back in my land of nostalgia. I had no place to go but back to my family. I wanted to live back closer to my mother. I missed her. My loving grandparents ended up taking me in for almost a year. I know it must have been sort of a hassle for me to live there but they would never tell me that. It was fun for that short time though. Although they were my grandparents, they weren't going to let me live there for free. It just so happened that the first job I applied for is the one I got. By this time I was having trouble with my foot while I was working at my duty station for the Marine Corp. A short time later I received a medical discharge. That's neither here nor there at this point. Again, we will come back to that.

Moving forwarding...I packed all my stuff from East Texas to move in with my Grandparents. This all happened so fast. The original reason to move was based on living with my girlfriend, which was closer for me being near to Momma. I digress. The better alternative to live with my grandparents came about because I found out that my girlfriend actually didn't have a place for us to live like she had promised. Meanwhile, in the process of moving, I pissed my brother off because I was moving away from home for a girl. Within a month I had moved to North Texas, got a well paying job, and settled everything with my family.

Blockbuster warehouse (Hey, remember Blockbuster?) called me in for orientation a week after I applied. A week and half after I went to orientation I met my possible new girlfriend. I know that sounds apprehensive. I get it.

Orientation was a blast because we had like twenty-five people that were all class clowns. (Except this one girl.) This one girl that was truly beautiful. She had the greatest personality. She was sweet. She spent the class laughing at all the other people. She looked shy and only seemed to only talk to the girl next to her. I made sure that I listened for her name when the class administrator called it. Her name was Misty. The whole time we were having this class, I couldn't help looking at her. I think she noticed me noticing her at the time. Of course, I am not shy and I don't grow timid. All I wanted was to talk to her. A few days later, she had passed me while we were working. I spoke up and said," Misty?! Smile, it becomes you!"

It seemed that I didn't want or need to be alone. I loved the fact that someone could be there for me. I wanted that companionship that I had always searched for. I pursued Misty for weeks. At times, I thought this woman wasn't at all interested in a guy like me. I just thought it was just another thing that I could toss it up to foolishness. I talked to her as often as I could, especially during breaks. Something drew me to her. I truly wanted to fall for this woman. Something inside told me that she would be safe for me to love.

We started having lunch together more often. We were talking one day and she was kind of timid in the way of telling me that she already had a little girl. I told her that it was awesome. She said she thought I was going to find a problem with it just like everyone else had. I thought it was great.

We started dating on March 21st of 1998. I met Chrissy about three weeks after. She was this cute little, blonde, blue-eyed short person that was only 2 ½ years at the time. She was so tiny. She was adorable and sweet.

The verdict was still out on when I was to meet her family, although her mother gave her a lot of hassle about not meeting me yet. It was the strangest thing that Chrissy only let Misty's dad hold her. It made my heart melt that when I first met her, I got to carry her into the house. It totally shocked Misty. Chrissy hardly spoke a word to any other person much less letting them hold her.

We were moving so fast in the relationship. I wasn't complaining. I was used to it after all the years of my companionships with all my exes. Not too far after I met Chrissy, I met the rest of her family. Her mother, beautiful for her age, had a youthfulness that I had never seen. She and Misty could've been twins. They almost sounded exactly alike on the phone. Her father was a big burley man with a full beard. He was the type that you didn't want to upset. She also had a little sister and a little brother. Her sister kind of kept to herself and her brother was active to say the least.

Within a month I had already proposed. She said yes! I really wanted this to happen. I had proposed to other women before but this time it was a more natural thing to do. I was surprised that the answer was positive. I was going through so much as far as emotions with my friends and family at the time. I was upset most of the time and just wanted her near me. I needed a listening ear. I didn't like the fact that I felt I was burdening her with all these issues, but she continued to listen. I kept talking.

We had a lot of hardships. I never expected us to but we tried to make the best of the worst of times. We had been engaged for about two years. Why so long? I haven't a clue. We finally set a date for the wedding and got everything we thought we needed. It was a simple wedding. It was all that I had hoped it would be. I felt happy that day. Despite of all the harsh feelings that I had for my some of people in my life, they showed up and I was emotionally overjoyed.

The wedding was fabulous and the reception was fun in all aspects. We told everyone that we were happy with the way things had gone. We told everyone thank you for coming. But, the one thing we didn't tell them is that Misty was about a month into pregnancy.

This is what I had wanted. I now had a family that I felt I was missing for most my life and now I had child of my own on the way. The only technicality was that Misty didn't want her family to know right away. It was mainly due to her father's high disappointment with her first pregnancy. At this time, I tried to explain the difference within the time span. Misty was a lot older now and her parents were possibly more suited to handle the news this time. Plus, I was more favorable in the eyes of her Misty's father than of the absentee "father" that had left Misty and Chrissy. Letting her parents know of our joy was obviously a bigger deal to me than it was to her. I just couldn't understand. So, needless to say, we spent a lot of time not speaking of the baby. This is something that tore at me. I was disgruntled in the way of the whole subject. It was supposed to be to a happy time in our lives, not one to be muffled due to the fact that her parents would feel disappointed again. I really wanted to let the world know and to talk about the baby freely but I couldn't.

Misty took her whole pregnancy in good stride. It wasn't at all what I had expected. She didn't have all the cravings that I have heard other women having. Did you know that some women crave dirt? I know right?! She dealt with the minor cramps better than I would have. All in all it was a smooth ride.

January 28, 2001 was the day we had to go to the hospital. She calmly came into the room and told me that we had to go right now. We got to the hospital and it took a while for the pregnancy to actually start. We were in the delivery room for about five hours. Everything was cool until Misty heard that she was going to have the baby right then and the doctor wasn't there. I mean the nurses are trained to do so as well, right? That was the only time I ever saw Misty freak out. It was understandably an emotional day. She got her tubes tied that day as well.

Around twenty-eight minutes after one, Katelynn was born! It was wonderful! We had brought this precious little girl into the world. Thank the Lord, she was healthy. She had what we thought to be, light brown hair and blue eyes. Come to find out, she had bright red hair. Red hair runs on Misty's side of the family. I have some trace of it but it was far down the line. She had a head full of hair though.

She was so cute! I was beginning to question if she was mine. (I kid! I joke! Come on laugh with me.) She was perfect! She was a little gift that I never expected to be so perfect. Now I felt proud like a father should feel. I could've flown away with only happiness to guide me. The day your child is born is one not ever to be forgotten.

Misty had become the one love I needed. She was the one I wanted for so long. She'd given me a loving place and a family I so desperately thought I needed.

Chapter Four

It's hard to wake up when the
shades have been pulled shut

There is a definite realism that is felt when it comes to family and friends. I felt it for nearly my entire young life. No one understood the things that went on within me. I confused myself.... sometimes. I felt out of place with my family. I was the foreign exchange student of the family. I don't understand why either. I was a good kid. I did the things that needed to be done to show my parents that I loved and respected them. I never quite understood why I had to endure these emotional wounds that weren't healing fast enough. My family was left out of most of the things that went on with me. My life experiences had surpassed the ones of anyone else my age and I was too young to deal with them on my own. This is the reason I spent a lot of time by myself.

I built my life around the fact of listening to people's problems. I felt I had to just to ignore my own. I still continue to do so at times. All anyone wants is to have someone that is neutral to vent to. On the other hand, I got tired of listening to all these issues and finding that no one was there to hear me. I guess people think that if you are the one that solves everyone's problems that you have none of your own. Some of this is my own fault for not communicating with my family upon the hurt I had endured.

Kerry Victor Jeffrey, the name bestowed unto my father and to which I got my first and last name, was thought to be a totally different person than I. A lot of his traits were installed in me. He is very calm most of the time and unemotional for the better part of his life. I have come to the conclusion that I will, in fact, never know my father as well as I have always wanted to. I am content with that. But I am left to feel that my dad is never going to know me for me. I love my dad more than he will ever know but most of the time I really needed a dad. It bothers me that he refuses to show any emotion and will not open up to me or my brother the way we want him to.

The separation between my mother and father dealt a heavier blow than I originally thought. It's not that I believe that the happenings between my parents truly messed me up for life. I will completely deny that. I think they are better off apart. I see where they both can drive each other crazy. They both had to move on to better themselves and us.

The blame is not upon my family. They are not the full cause of all the depressing emotions that I lived with everyday. I'm not sure where it all started. I hated myself for all the sadness and rage. Why was I so different? Was this the real me? I couldn't escape myself. I would've given anything to live in someone else's shoes. Some of my friend's lives seemed to be perfect.

My family wasn't a bad one. They were good. I mean it could have been a lot worse. I believe that I was misunderstood a lot of the time. They say never blame yourself for things that are out of your control. I did though. I blamed myself for the communication break down between me and my father. As if I wasn't trying hard enough on some level. I envied the guys that could talk to their fathers. It was like something out of some movie that had the same life issues. I waited for the major life event that was supposed to happen to bring me and my dad together. But let's face it; life is nothing like an after school special.

It's funny that it's hard to believe that they never wondered what was going on with me unless I expressed it through being really emotional. I don't express much to family. I know they care about me. I feel I am always wrong with them. They do care about me but I always seemed a burden to them if ever I had a problem. I'm guessing that's why I don't share a lot with too many people. I figure they could care less. I am guilty of putting myself into that box.

All those years, you think that you'll never be like your family. You stand at the crossroads. You don't know which path to choose. If you are too close to the family you love, you end up like them. If you deny them, they end up rejecting you. It's a hard lesson learned that no matter which path you chose, your family and their characteristics will be with you, inside that heart of yours, always.

Chapter Five

Hearts and thoughts they fade

fade away

Okay, back on track. (1991!) Seventh grade was when the big move to east Texas took place. The next four years didn't have much importance in the context of these writings. The major things that happened were I had a couple of bad relationships, embarrassed myself a lot, managed to make some friends with a few guys, tripped on shrooms for two hours of school thanks to one of those friends, got felt up with a foot massage to the groin during gym, beat up while in gym, and of course, me and a guy named William caught a glimpse of a sexy teachers panties with her in them. Well, that about covers the exciting part of those four years. The rest of the time I spent in my room writing and suffering from my so called syndrome.

Junior year was a time I started pointing my interests towards younger women.   (Not too young, Geez!) I thought maybe they would keep me company longer because they would stay interested longer. They always said that a woman always looks for an older man anyways (That being a positive for me). Plus older guys know more and have more resources. I didn't, but I digress.

I guess it all started when my sister showed me a picture of this girl she was friends with. I thought she was cute, but for the time being I had my own problems with Kendra that had just broke up with me for the second time. Needless to say, I was interested. One year had lapsed before I even talked to girls. She knew who I was because of my sister and ditto on my part. I was sort of interested in this other girl at the time. Really no need to mention her name. She was a tad on the psycho side. Anyway, I went to this dance and that's where I met her. We ended up dancing the whole night, but Tabatha tried to get me to notice her. (Oh, sorry I didn't mention that before.) Her name was Tabatha. No need to give the last name. That night, I guess all gears were stuck on stupid! The little psycho and I dated for only a week. (I hope that wasn't too confusing.)

We broke up on a Thursday, so I had all weekend to mope around the house. Monday rolled around and the first person I saw was Tabatha. She wasn't single at the time, but I didn't care. I could still talk to her. I told her hello and made her laugh a little bit. She introduced me to her boyfriend at the time. I don't remember his real name but everyone called him Doorknob. I still think that's funny. I don't know why. She broke up with him within two days and she made it a point to tell me she was single. (Note taken!) A day and half later, we were a couple.

We spent every chance; every waking moment either talking to one another or smothering each other. I was content in this time in my life. I spent time with her and her family. Her family loved me and even offered me choices that I didn't have with my family. Such things as helping to get financial aid started for school and teaching me how to drive a little better. I learned a lot about love and life from her family. I loved her more than anything at that time.

After I graduated I started thinking about my education and thought the armed services would be a good idea. Right before the time I was to leave for the Marine Corp, I made it a point to visit my mom and grandparents. Problem was that Kendra still lived a couple of miles away. Needless to say, things got out of hand and Kendra and I ended up kissing and I let it go on for a little too long. It was long enough to make me feel absolutely terrible about what pain I just caused Tabatha and myself as well. I went back and called to tell her what had happened. We broke up two weeks before I had to leave for boot camp. Which, if that hadn't taken place, I had the opportunity to decline the service. I loved her and yet my depression caused me to withdraw my feelings for her. I just wanted her. I also left Kendra at a standstill because I left without telling her goodbye. I always told her that if anything happened where I couldn't take it anymore in East Texas, I would move in with her and possibly get married. I was ready to wed when I was eighteen because I felt marriage brought the love I deserved.

The night before I had to leave, Tabatha called me. She was saddened at the fact that I was leaving, but somewhere hidden under the tender voice was the realization that I had still hurt her. I told her I would miss her, I would write, and I would see her soon.

Boot camp was spent very lonely due to the fact that the only people I had to write to were family. So, I took a chance one day and wrote Tabitha a letter which said that I hadn't spent a day not thinking of her. She wrote back and told me she loved me and would like to get back together. So we did. I don't remember much of boot camp after that day. Before I left the base, after the graduation ceremony, I bought her a ring. I didn't give Kendra another thought. For some reason I thought she had forgotten about me.

In the back of my mind I thought, "Wouldn't it be great if Tabatha was there?" There to meet me when I got off the plane?" I got off the plane in Texas, Tyler to be exact, and my family was so proud to see me. I looked at my family, (that I actually missed), and asked, "Where is she?" I knew at that moment she had to be there. She was! My family made it a point to have her there. On the way home, I asked her to marry me and she agreed.

Sadly, we only spent six more months together. Only then did I realize that I had truly fell in love with a person that understood the way I thought, the way I acted, and the way I had dreamt. Maybe she'll understand a little more of what I was thinking upon reading this.

I'm not quite sure what went wrong in the relationship but looking back I am only to guess. Maybe she was looking for stability or maturity. Both of which I did not have. She did make me happy though. Maybe she was just one those lights that I simply smothered away. It seemed to be a trend. It was so stupid to let my self esteem take root and not let me move further.

The last part of our relationship was spent arguing and misinterpreting each other, so we sort of agreed that we should split and mutually go our separate ways. Before the courtship ended, I went to a county fair and met up with some friends there. I think..! Maybe I'm a little fuzzy on that detail. Anyway...I ran into another one of Tabatha's friends. Her name was Melissa. That night, I felt so relaxed talking to her (like we had been friends forever). Of course, I was always so easy to talk to anyway. It was like she knew my walls were crumbling. She was there to help me pick up the pieces of tattered emotions that were falling to the bottom of my heart. I just thought I would take the time to thank her for that. For some reason we never went out with each other. I think I've kicked myself a few times on that note. Thanks for listening Melissa.

I know this chapter is kind of confusing. I think I have explained it the simplest as I could.

Chapter Six

Up ahead, in the distance

I saw a shimmering light

(1997) So, graduation had come and gone. Marine Corp training was done. (Still don't wanna talk about it.)

After I got out of boot camp, my brother Corry and I decided to move into a house together in the little town we had grew up in through our teenage years. He had decided to move back because he had moved away for some time to live with our mother in North Texas. I'm glad he came back. We had found a house in town that was only three hundred a month. It was great except for the fact that we had the bitchiest landlord on the face of the planet. It was home for the time being.

We were both doing well holding down night jobs at Denny's. (It's sad I know.) I was going to my duty station once a month in accordance to my contract I had with the Marine Corp, but I did not like it.

One Monday night, after I got back from the reserve base, I and my friends went to this pizza place kind of outside of town. We were just goofing around and for the most part just having fun. I had heard that Mandy's mother worked there (Mandy- Reference last part of chapter two). We wanted to go there for the simple reason that the place had a pool table. So, as we were going in, Mandy was rushing out. I didn't notice who was rushing past me at first, but she noticed me and stopped in her tracks.

We spent some time together at the pizza place and again at my friend James' house. That is when I kissed her for the first time. It was getting late that night and we decided to go to my house. My friend Bill and his sister Katie offered to drive because I didn't have a car at the time. The four of us spent about two hours hanging out, joking, and remembering the old days of school. Mandy ended up spending the night that night. I thought it was just as good a time as any. Angels sung that night because I finally got the one girl I had pretty much lusted over for so long.

My family didn't really like her at all but maybe that was the point. I adored her. Let's just say that most of my girlfriends weren't too favorable (basically because I only wanted most of them as companions). She was different though. I guess it was because I had longed for her for so long. I was willing to do anything for this girl. I only promised her the things I knew would eventually make her happy and things that were obtainable. I loved the fact that she was there. My only purpose was to make her happy. I may have over done it at times though. I say this because I was never sure she felt the same about me. Sadly, our relationship didn't go as smoothly as I thought it would go. All I wanted for her was to show her a better life. A life I wanted for her, with me.

Mandy had a lot of things to sort out in her life. I naturally wanted to help her in what I thought was a cure. She was so dependent on drugs and attention. I forgave her too many times. The last I heard from her was when we broke up. I was supposed to move in with her, which failed terribly. She called me two weeks later and broke it off. That is how I finally got out of East Texas and stranded myself in North Texas in order to be closer to my mother and grandparents. She called me a month later and tried to apologize, but I didn't want to hear it. It did feel good to shove her off one last time, but it tugged at my heart strings just a little to tell her that I was better off without her. I didn't feel as if it was the truth at the time but I needed to let her know that I was hurt. The last time I heard anything of Mandy was that she was married with children and happy. I hope she's okay.

They say it's possible to fall in lust and looking back...maybe it was just that. I wanted to love her so completely in my efforts. Although, it wasn't lust. I did feel more than the common admiration for this girl. I wanted to marry her.

After the fall of Mandy, I was fearful in wanting to date another blonde. I think they confused me more than anything. They are good to look at though. She was my first sexual experience. That is possibly why I wanted it to work. But she is someone I will always remember. Maybe I'll find the heart to talk to her again one day. The one thing I did learn from her was that trying to make others happy for your own happiness was never meant to work as well as you plan. But it was the only thing I knew how to do. That's what I call being a stranger to my own reality.

Chapter Seven

My love will laugh with me
before the morning comes

My dark tunnel was the null, yet full void in which my version of depression called home. Did I really want this? Did I want this thing that was reality but in reality made me sick? Am I the outcast? Am I really okay? Am I actually loved or am I just another spot of light in someone else's dark world? I used to question things like these and others. I questioned a lot of things. Maybe sometimes, in the sub-text, I still do.

When my parents went their separate ways, it was something that affected us all. Families are there to support each other. It's not the fact that two people, upon one single decision, can utterly rip that moral strand in half. I always felt that my family loved me but they really didn't know who I was. That is why I felt I had to look for love and companionship in other people.

At age eleven, after the separation, after the actual divorce, and all things mundane, Dad received custody of all three of us. Mom was left to lead the life she dreamt of but contracted a few unfavorable boyfriends. All we got was some lousy visitations and years to wonder what really happened. Needless to say, Mom moved away and Dad suffered to make ends meet with three kids, one job, and a house that was falling apart. We grew up poor, but I was never ashamed of that fact. We grew up thankful for what we had. We were content with what we had. We never knew any different.

Things didn't start to affect me until the teenage years. I didn't feel loved or cared for. My teenage years were spent very lonely. I say that sadly. I spent several years inside the confines of my own denial. The only thing that kept me occupied was school and the little time I got to spend with friends. Thank God for friends!

As I've said, part of my problem came from the fact that me and my father never communicated. I was never the one to talk about anything that was bothering me to the same sex. I can talk all day to a woman, which isn't unheard of these days. My father is not an emotional type of person. Or so they say. I wouldn't know. It still hurts me that he has no motivation to come and see me every once in a while. I would think he would like to see if I am alive every once in a blue moon. Me and him are too much alike. It's true what they say. The one you fight with the most is the one most like you.

Don't get me wrong, I love my family. But it is a different love that I never expected. It is different than the admiration I had as when I was young and naive. I was always the odd man out. No matter what I did, it never seemed to be as important as what my brother and sister could achieve. As I think back, every major decision I made was vetoed by someone. The decision to graduate early (or on time to correctly put it) and the option to join the services wasn't a joyful conversation. At one point, I started hiding <u>all</u> of my feelings towards my family. I felt this hopelessness towards anything I thought was right.

When I was seventeen, I thought about death a lot. I guess that's why I'm not really afraid of the after-life like all those times before. I read a lot of books about after death experiences and dreamt about a lot of morbid things that I care not to revisit. In my dreams, my mind was tragically wasted away too many times to count.

I don't know what changed but somewhere along the way I figured that life was too important to miss. This is when this book started to form more meaningful words.

Over the years, I have found out that a lot of rage has built up inside. I am not a person that lets that rage out normally. I don't like to take my anger out on anyone whether they are to blame for that anger or not.

All these years, I have taken all this rage and put it away deep inside. I know it's hurtful but I really didn't want to hurt the ones I loved either.

As I've said before, I believe depression is incurable. It's just one of those things in life that sticks with you. There are a lot of ways to subdue it, but it never leaves. To this day, I still look for a way to find the better man within. If I can't find it in myself, maybe I have to see strength in others.

Now, they say that depression hurts more than the mind. That it can cause you a lot of physical pain. Damn, that explains a lot. It explains the fact that some days I feel like crap for no reason at all. So it leads me to believe that if the heart breaks too many times, it can ultimately destroy you. I am determined that this will not ever destroy me.

Chapter Eight

I watched a change in you

It's like you never had wings

I've always known how to draw and to write poetry. It has been a huge part of my life and quite possibly always will. I didn't want to put art work in this book but I can give my poetry its dues. I used to write all the time. Poetry relaxes me for some odd reason.

So this chapter is going to be chopped full of it. Here's how it is going to go. I will write a piece for you and in turn interpret it so that you'll understand why I wrote it. That's way more than you get from most poets.

Illness-

My life, now and forever, will be just a blanketed expression of love for which I was meant to see. Something great.

My soul, now and forever, will be just a confused immoral idea that I have led myself to believe. Something's out there.

My body, now and forever, will be just a statue of a divine figure that's truly sad but doesn't know how to show it. Some things remain the same.

Depression at its worst. No self esteem and no idea where I was going or where I'd end up.

First Loves-

First loves, Feelings of pain. Just mere shadows, Of distant rain.

To the rain, I've made a fire, In which to ravish my desire. If we were together, I'd hardly tire.

Thoughts of doubt, Things I've left out. Hurt and anguish. What's this love all about?

This reflects my school days when I had such a heavy crush on one of my friends. I tried so hard to get her to notice me and all I did was cry for her.

If....?-

If a friend was a lover, It would be a thought.

To have someone there, more often than not.

Now this was the interesting part of my life. It took me three years to actually be in a relationship. It states just what I was thinking at the time. I had a crush; enough said.

What's the matter?-

What's the matter now? Is it you or is it me?

There must be something, That makes our hearts growl.

Is it hurt or hunger, That makes us prowl?

What's the matter with us, that we can't love one another?

Why can't we live peacefully, With nothing to bother?

What's the matter with them? They cause trouble; they're tormented.

They think wrong; Emotions they make are demented.

What's the matter with me? I seek love, that's all;

I hurt so much. I hurt from the fall.

Basically, I trusted no one. I was living on experience alone, but I was still leery of people hurting me. To me, everything in my life was going the wrong direction.

Alone-

Alone at the end of nothing, The lights have faded in face to blue. Emotions poised on every aspect, All I ever wanted was you.

We were up all night, Tearing our loves apart. Now it was plain to see, The love wasn't in my heart.

And I'm a liar to you! I was shown the light, But I turned away. Never knew love was such a fight.

This was to the first girl that I tried to love but I needed as a friend more. I felt very isolated towards myself and others. I needed someone there so I felt needed.

Hell-

Wicked feelings, evil thoughts, It's what you get when religion is lost- South of Heaven, fires grow, Do wrong here; you're in for a show. No one wants to be there, but often souls are, Being left with a burden, an eternal scar.

Religion is a big thing to me. Even though I don't get to church as often as I need to, I still have a strong believe in the Lord.

You & I-

I see you through my eyes of hurting,

For like the lion, I search for something.

I wait in great desperation,

For the world is causing my frustration.

I see you through my eyes of caring,

For like the cub, I strive for more.

I see the world different, with little vision,

For the sun does rise and rain does pour.

You see me through your eyes of glitter,

For like the lioness, you see things precious.

You wait with all your wonder,

For you are the rain, yet the thunder.

That was the one I originally wrote for Misty.

When I was younger, I never really used my art work as much as the poetry. I only drew when I was really bored or when I really had the craving to do so. You should have seen my book covers in school. If my head wasn't in the book, you could bet my pen was doodling on it.

I used poetry to express my feelings through writing; just hoping someone would want to read it.

Stereo Typical-

300 eyes staring upon my shadow

Looking upon in disarray

My thoughts become empty

Why does the corrupt stay?

Thoughts of hurt are acid

They rot my moral chain

The negatives sub-due positive

But emotions care to complain.

 Breathe in for I am air

Wonderful as a star

Why don't others see me

As common as they are?

Basically, I was tired of being judged and had really low self esteem at the time.

Turtles-

Ever watch a turtle

So lonely; so slow?

Doesn't really do much

Doesn't put on a show!

He has that tough shell

That makes it hard to walk.

Does he speak a word

Does he ever talk?

I guess he doesn't do much

Just simple daily habits.

Except for when he races

Those quick silly rabbits!

On occasion, I write funny poems as well.

There is so much more poetry than this. I have been writing it longer than I have been writing this. I just wanted to show you as a reader that I could write things that were meaningful and how I expressed those things years ago. I think most anything I have put down on paper has or had a meaning. Poetry was my way of being someone.

Chapter Nine

Tell me all your

thoughts on God

Religion as far as going to a public building and showing that I believe in the almighty one never really made sense to me. I mean that I did need to show the world that I believed. I knew God was there; I knew the love was there. Religion in my everyday life is a big part of me. There is still a lot to which I don't understand about the word but I'm learning. Some may ask why a chapter about religion? Why not? It helped me. That's the only reason. We always went to church when we were young. We were never pushed to go. But we knew of what religion was. We never had a base religion. We were a part of many different ones. We visited Baptist, Catholic, Methodist, and Episcopalian. We just went to be around people our own age. It got us out of the house. I never understood the part of the belief that you try to get saved. Didn't Jesus save us when he died for all people to save us from our sins? I'm not going into a big religious discussion over what I believe and what others think is right compared to the Holy Bible. I have just a few things to mention. Maybe a few questions, also.

I had a step-grandfather that was very wise and joyful for what I saw of him. A man that lived his life with all he had been given and made do with what he had. My step mom shows a lot of what he had taught her. I remember that we used to play in the nearby creeks and walked along the railroad tracks when we visited. We had moved away from the country so we liked to do things like that. I have some good memories from that place.

I remember he had to remain in the hospital for quite a bit of time when he got emphysema. He was on a breathing machine for a long time. I had to learn that emphysema is a disease, in which the alveoli of the lungs become stretched to an excessive degree and lose their elasticity, resulting in an often-severe loss of breathing ability. It is caused by smoke inhalation (Cigarette and cigar smoking being the most common destroying factor). Okay, enough with the facts of the matter.

Paul Fultz was my grandfather's name. He was a step grandfather, but nonetheless. Everyone called him Peepaw as well as I. He was very sick at the very last. I prayed for him and then everything else every night. So, when he was in the hospital, many people came to visit. One of which was the Pastor of our church. On day, on one of the Father's many visits, my grandfather, talked to him in a very low tone. He said, "Father? I've never been much of a religious man. So, when you talk to your boss, will you tell him that I love him?" That pulled at my heartstrings a little and made me realize what kind of man he actually was. He was the kind of man that believed but didn't have to tell everyone that he did so.

There are so many things that are meant to be questioned with religion. Like the fact that we make mistakes everyday and the Lord lets us. (Because we learn by trial and error.) For the many trails that we go through in life, it is nothing compared to the perils that the Lord suffered for us. A little boy made me realize something a long time ago. We were talking about cartoons and he asked how they are made. I conveyed my interest in the subject by telling him what I knew about how to create them. After I had finished, he asked if God drew us. (Touché') He had a good point. Who is behind the animation? God put us here for good reasons. It's the reasons that we don't understand all the time.

I chose to write this part because it held importance to me. I trusted in the Lord to keep me safe.

Chapter Ten

Teach me how to speak
Teach me how to share

For motivational and venting purposes only, I am choosing to share some of my memories. It's said that listing things like memories and past experiences is good for a healthy emotional wellbeing.

I remember....

...the time that I fell in love for the first time.

...that when I was eighteen, someone finally spoke up and said, "I'm proud of you".

...being bullied in school because I was different.

...the first time a movie actually made me cry.

...the feeling I felt when I learned that I could make someone laugh.

...my first fight. I lost.

...the first feeling of depression and wondering what the hell it was.

...the first time I really felt abandoned.

...my first trip I took away from Texas. Just me and Dad.

...when I first started smoking.

...when we were poor but never hungry. (Thanks Dad!)

...the time I went to Disney World.

...that I have never been really close to my siblings.

...taking a ride in a laundry mat's dryer.

...when someone told me that they loved me and I believed her.

...when Dad remarried for the better.

...when Momma remarried for what she thought was the better.

...the thoughts of hurt and anger with depression.

...when my brother left to move in with mom.

...my first kiss.

...my first real kiss.

...when I moved away from my parent's house.

...my first rent house and much alcohol passed through it.

...how bad it really was in boot camp.

...when I first cheated on someone and how bad it felt.

...when my friends took their lives. (God Bless You Bill and Tasha)

...feeling unwanted all the time.

...the day I got my license. (I was twenty.)

...the day I got a ticket for running a light.

...meeting my future wife.

...meeting my first daughter.

...the first moment I realized I was a dad.

...meeting my future in-laws. (What a riot.)

...the divorce.

...when I felt like a had a best friend (Love you Holly).

...when I fell for the younger girl.

...the first time my heart really broke.

These aren't in any particular order. I just randomly selected from memory. That last one is quite possibly why I chose to write a book of this caliber though. Thanks for letting me express things.

I know people say not to let the past rule your present. If you let it, it will consume you. I know it's such a needless thing to do. I believe God gave us the gift of memory so we learn from it. Maybe it keeps our hearts safe in so many ways. It's hard to move away from it though....sometimes. It's hard to see past the tears sometimes. I try to forget. Sometimes I wish the hurt would simply vanish. I don't care to know where it goes. I imagine it could just blow away.

Chapter Eleven

I told dirty jokes

until you smiled

Comedy has always been my defense mechanism. I've always found the simplest things funny. You know...tears of a clown...

I used to hear the phrase, "You should've been a comedian! I think you missed your calling" all the time. Humor has always been the very best medicine for me.

You ever wonder if Eve never bit the apple? Have you thought how that would've changed things? We would just be walking around stark naked. You wouldn't have to ask any stupid questions, I'll tell you that much. Questions like, "Honey, are you cold?" or "Hey man you think she's hot?" and best of all, "Hey Honey? You think she's pretty?", they just wouldn't exist.

I think sex is funny. Not to begin this uncomfortably, but I grew up in a time when sex wasn't talked about much and the internet wasn't a thing yet. We learned the reproductive system in health class. Then it was all downhill from there. We had Sports Illustrated, our imaginations, and if we were lucky our dad had a magazine stash. Those were the good old days of being curious and yet having the fear you'd get caught.

Yeah, in class, we learned the important stuff. We started out laughing about words like masturbation, ejaculation, and why we should refer to as sperm; not the other choice words for it . We learned important things like, within intercourse, the sperm enters a woman's body by the millions, yet only about fifty make it to the fertile egg.

The funny part is the situation of the moment. To me, it seems that there is a massive blowout party and every guy that is capable is going to see the striper. The problem is that it is such a long trip just to get there. Now, on the way there, 999,999,950 guys stop because they are out of gas. The fifty that are left actually get to the party and have a great time. Then, about the middle of the party, Forty-nine of the guys get pissed off because the one guy that scored with the striper is the dork of the group.

Love is funny too. It's the only thing in the world that makes teens practice kissing in the mirror and making out with their arms. Hickey!! How is that a word for bruised skin? Love makes you do crazy things. Like wearing favored massage oil or edible underwear. The only thing that stuff got me is a sticky ass. But, that may be a story for another time or another book all together.

Pardon me if I go from one extreme to the other from time to time. So, here's a question..! If your road gets a new layer of asphalt, is it a retard road? My sister wrote a letter to a former camp counselor in which it stated (and I'm not kidding) "We just got our roads retard." She is constantly being funny when she doesn't realize it.

My brother was always skinnier than I was and still is. He used to make comments about my weight. By definition, I was just a little chunkier than him. You know how siblings try to get the better of each other. One day our great uncle told him that if he ever fell from something high he would hurt himself. On the other hand, I would bounce a couple of times and be alright. A short time later, we were trying to build a tree house in a twelve foot tree. Although he swears I pushed him accidentally, my brother fell out from where he was. I swear he did a flip in mid-air. He landed on his chest, facing the ground. It was like comparing play-dough to silly putty. Like clay, he didn't bounce. As things turned out we both ended up with head to toe poison ivy. He got to spend some rather long days in the hospital. The dark humor about this is that as soon as he hit the ground, I said to myself, "Bounce!"

Although I got no credit for it, I was the original person that said, "That's what she said!" Just trust me. My family knows the story of how my step-mom got upset at me while at the dinner table when she asked Dad why he didn't give her more meat.

Mom had a tough time with four guys in the house. I'm surprised that my mouth didn't get me in even more trouble for the next thing I'm going to tell you. Mom was trying to tell us that her and my younger brother installed the child safety latches earlier on in the day. She explained that it took an hour for them to install one safety device and it only needed two screws to install. I spoke up without thinking and said," Oh, thirty minutes a screw, huh?" Upon hearing this, my brother busted out laughing, nearly spitting his food halfway across the table. Then Dad caught on a second later, then my sister; then Mom.

So, I was watching Channel 13 (PBS). You know the one that has support from all the viewers like you. This is what I learned. The North American tree frog's tadpoles only fear in life is an ugly green bug that eats them for the nourishment of its own unborn spawn. This bug dives under the water and waits. When it catches one of these tadpoles, it kills it, eats it, and throws it aside. Little does he know that when he bites into this young amphibian, it releases a strange chemical. This chemical released into the water warns the other tadpoles to stay away from this area. So, this chemical initiates a gene inside of the other tadpoles. It enhances them so that their tails get stronger, increases their body mass, and discolors their tails to look bright red. This lets them get away from this bug faster than they could before. Now, you're asking," What the hell is he rambling on about?" So, I'm sitting there watching this in full amazement and thinking only one thing. "Well, I'll be damned. Frogs have menstrual cycles!"

Does a reptile know when it loses its tail? Does he go home after spending a long night with the guys to his little lizard den, steps halfway into the door, and says, "Honey, I lost my ass tonight!?" She promptly responds, "I bet you did. I told you not play poker with the snakes!" By this time he steps into the door, turns around and says pointing to his backside, "No, seriously!" She's like, "Crap! Not again!"

I think we need more big people in commercials. For example, that old Taco Bell commercial when they come out and yell, "I'm full!" I would have eaten a lot more Taco Bell if a fat guy was in that commercial. (Seriously) If I would have seen a big guy, about two hundred pounds, step out and yell, "I'M FULL!" I'd be like, "I'm going to Taco Bell! They filled that guy up. We gotta go right now."

In Texas, we get salamanders and geckos around the house all the time. A friend text messaged me once and said that she was afraid to go into the laundry room because there was a gecko in there. I asked her if she could catch it for me. She said that she wasn't going near it because she was scared the death of them. I told her that if she could catch it she could save at least 15% or more on her car insurance. I had a good laugh anyway.

I have always liked meatier, healthier girls. Seeing a skinny girl wasn't attractive to me. I asked a good buddy why he thought I was attracted to only them. He said that it's all a part of attraction. So I asked him and I quote, "So, you think I'm Bounty?" He replies, "What?" I say, "You know? The quicker, thicker, picker upper?"

A friend once told me he had this girlfriend that became a lesbian. She always came home drunk saying that she just got messed up with gin and brandy. Yeah, come to find out that gin was short for Jennifer and brandy was spelled with an "I". That conversation went from alcohol to lesbianism in about 5.2 seconds.

I try to think about funny stuff all the time. They say that some of the truest saddest stuff in life makes a great comedy routine. Sometimes I think too much.

I think it would be funny to scotch guard the soap and watch someone try to wash with it. They would find it real hard to get the damn thing to produce a lather. Wouldn't you think?

I thought about writing one those how to "dummy" books. I think I would make a lot of money writing one too! I would call it- Wipe your ass for dummies. The first page would have step by step instructions on how one would go about doing this chore and the rest of the pages you could use to do the duty.

That's it! I am writing a comedy book later on. By the time, I get this published I'll probably have one written. Go ahead; go look for it. I am sure it's out there.

Chapter Twelve

...you're already the

voice inside my head

I am the type of person that could make a friend at any time. I like that fact. Friendships over the years kept me sane. When it came to friends, the ratio was about three girls to one guy actually being a friend. I loved having friends that were female. These days that means you're stereotyped as being gay. I am far from that. My emotions are scared and feeble but I absolutely love women. They encouraged the companionship I felt I needed. I think my mother moving away and my father not being around played a tremendous part in that. I wanted someone there to understand me and for the most part take care of me. My friends took care of the parts I was missing from my family. My friends were my family.

Although I hid a lot of my problems, I was the first person they ran to if they had one. This is how I felt needed. I figured this was my place in the world, to just simply lend an ear. I loved my friends. I loved them for who they were. I loved the fact that they were there for me.

I always planned on mentioning all my friends in this book but I began to write them down and thought maybe not. All my friends, past and present, know I mean well. I'm sorry!!! There are a lot of you to mention but thank you all. I do want you to know that all my friends are a big part of my life and this book.

I lost two good friends to suicide. I hate to think of it sometimes. I miss them. Their memory helps me try to finish this book that has taken so long to write.

Bill J. was just one of the good ole boys. He was simple in the way he lead his life. Sometimes, for the lack of targets, he would shoot cans or bottles among other things he found in his yard. He was a country boy at heart. But for the most part he liked to be in the company of his friends. He was always up for a good time or a good party. He was a little brother. He liked to laugh. I talked to him about life and love most of the time. Looking back I can see where Bill had a lot of thoughts just as I did. It seems he had a lot of sadness he was hiding also. That is something we never talked about though. I mean we semi-ignored the signs sometimes. I would've liked to help.

The signs started revealing themselves when Bill called another one of our mutual friends one night while we were all just hanging out and said he was in the hospital. Of course, we were all really concerned until we found out why. He had tried to overdose on aspirin. I don't remember ever being that mad and concerned at the same time. The story behind it was that I had asked the girl he liked to marry me the day before. It was all an attempt to get back at Mandy at the time. She had cheated on me like four times. It was my time to make her feel like shit. Little did I know that it would back fire the way it did. She told me no anyway that night before he called. Bill got out of the hospital and none of us ever mentioned the occasion again.

Less than three months later, Mandy left me in north Texas due to the fact that she didn't have a place for us to live. I only saw Bill one more time. I had come to visit Dad with my new fiancé when I decided to call my friends and see what they were up to. They wanted to come and visit me at Dads. They actually wanted me to join them at a party. I couldn't leave my fiancé at my parents' house just to go party. So we visited for a little more than an hour that night. I told Bill that I would have to come back to visit again soon. I never got back to visit Bill. I wish I had.

It was late one night when my friend Claudia called me with the news. She asked me if I had heard about Bill. Of course, I said no. Bill had taken his own life due to heartbreak from a girl. It was a pain I all knew too well. He had shot himself two days before. It was my other friend that found him. I broke down then. I told her I couldn't make it to the funeral the next day but I would find a way to say goodbye. This section of this book was my way of saying goodbye. Bill was my friend that was kind of like a soul mate. I tortured myself after his death with regret. I could have been there more for him. Just to let him know that I knew how it was and how it could be. But could I have helped at that point. I think about it constantly. I miss Bill. The world lost one hell of a guy. I knew it as well as anyone.

Tasha M. is the other friend that I miss. She was a girlfriend of mine for about two weeks. She was one of the youngest at the time. Tasha was one of the cutest of all my girlfriends. She was so petite compared to a lot of my girlfriends prior. We met at some sort of festival that was near my house that year. The relationship would have lasted longer if her dad didn't have a problem with his daughter actually having a boyfriend and if I would have known ahead of time about how Mandy was. I broke up with Tasha due to the fact that I had feelings for Mandy all those years. I only got to see her once more before see passed away. I and a couple of friends of mine went to visit her one night after we found out she had broke her leg. It wasn't even a long visit at the time. I told her that I was sorry for my prior actions and she forgave me. I missed her. She was a great friend and an even greater girlfriend. Her dad wasn't very happy we actually dated. Age difference was a big deal. She was still only barely sixteen when we met. Needless to say I wasn't. Her father was due home at any time, so we had to cut the visit short.

Sometime later after Bill died, I got a call from Dad and Mom. Mom told me that Tasha had passed away. A little bit after I left east Texas to be with Mandy, Tasha's father became severely ill. Tasha was taken care of him, her brother, and trying to maintain her own life. They said she had so much stress that she was suffering from bad migraines. She was taken a high medication for the headaches. It just so happened that she accidentally forgot that see already took the dosage she needed. She overdosed with just those few pills. I don't remember how old she was but she was younger than eighteen at the time. Now, all of this was told to me second hand so don't quote me fully of the details of the whole incident. Love you Tasha.

God bless you both, Bill and Tasha!

Chapter Thirteen

Why does love always
feel like a battlefield

Okay, now we fast forward to 2007. I know this gap is a big one.

I never said that I was emotionally sound in the way of my own well being. Misty and I spent some silent years just trying to figure out how we differed. I was an open book and she wasn't. I didn't blame her for it. It was how she was taught. It didn't help the matter when she told me to not try to figure her out because she would change if I did. I did it well. I lived everyday as if it were the first. I showed her that I wanted to be there with her. I cared for this woman along with her child that I had taken as my own along with my own daughter. We got along as well as we could.

I worked as hard as possible like my dad had always showed his children. I had many jobs. I had too many to count at the moment. I was never happy at one particular job. I kept food on the table and the rent stayed current. When I was without that stability, Misty worked with her mother to keep up. We had our share of the hard times.

I spent many years upset due to the fact that the only family I felt I had was Misty and the girls. Dad worked all his life to keep us healthy and sheltered. I love him for it. I got upset that he never called or wrote. It truly broke my heart worse than anything that I felt that I had a father who didn't seem to want to show me he loved me. I still sometimes believe he doesn't really know how. I can't blame him. He grew up that way. There was one incident when Misty and I first lived together. This was way before the time of Katelynn. I got really upset at the fact that my family wouldn't call or even show himself every once in a while. I was proud to have the support of my little family. I wanted my Dad to be a part of my life and to me it just felt as if he didn't have the time. Needless to say, this was the first of many things that affected my relationship thus far with my family. The way I looked at it is that I had this damn roller coaster of emotions all my life and no one seemed to want to help me where I needed it. I needed the love of my family and Dad's emotional support at that time in my life.

It was one of those things that I felt I never had but brutally missed. Please don't get me wrong in the fact that Dad does love his kids. He gave us the life he could with what he could give us. I love him for the very fact that he worked to keep us alive.

Many years went by and many fights ensued. I was getting frustrated at the fact that my whole perception of what a family is supposed to be was really tainted. I was fighting with my parents because they never came to visit or called, etc. They were angry with Misty because she was voicing her opinion in my defense. My dad and I stayed irritated at each other for it seems like forever. It was all holding a heavy strain upon me. I was fighting for just someone to listen but no one was. I tried so hard to make things right but in turn something angry was always drudged up again. The woman I trusted with everything in my life wouldn't listen to what I was trying to say. She made a bad choice in the friends she chose at the time. I told her that they were not the type of people she needed to be around but I was again ignored. It seemed very unreasonable for me to even have an opinion at the time. Her take on the subject of her new friends was that these people were the first real friends she had in a while so she didn't feel the need to forget them.

Misty always said that she always understood me in the way I felt. I disagreed with that point. It is hard to understand a situation if in turn you haven't been through it yourself. Her parents never divorced and she never experienced the shit I, my brother, and sister had to go through to get this far.

To make things worse, Misty and I were fighting all the time. We fought over the stupidest crap. I would never talk to her about the problems that I had with my family. I got more irritated that she always down-graded me that I didn't talk to her about every single thing. Why should I have talked to people about the issues I had if I felt no one understood or for that matter even listened to me? My issues were my problems. I didn't feel the need to be a burden to the ones I loved. It was so much easier just to hide it and keep it to myself.

Eventually Misty got tired of me not talking or paying enough attention to her and started to voice that the marriage isn't going to work if I do not communicate with her. She made some pretty awful statements throughout the course of all the endless talks and all I could do is to tell her that I was okay and to not leave me. Not getting all these problems out lead to the demise of the relationship. She asked me to leave one night and I did. Whether she meant for us to take a break from each other for a while or not, she just told me to leave. To me this was the end of the relationship as far as us being together was concerned. The basis of the whole thing was she felt that I didn't love her any longer. That wasn't the fact that made me leave that night. It hurt so badly that someone actually told me to leave.

I had a lot of things to carry on my shoulders and really didn't want to burden anyone else with all the issues I was facing. My issues within myself were to be dealt with by me and me alone. I could not disregard or disengage all the feelings I was having at the time. It may have been the case that I didn't feel I could've loved Misty as well as she loved me. If she loved me as much as she said she did, why did she push me into the negative?

I hesitated packing my stuff but I knew for me I had to go. It wasn't so much as her giving me a way out than as it was the feeling of not being loved by anyone. I knew that to better myself I had to change. I was betraying my own self in the way I saw myself. The old me would've stayed that night and fought until the last tear drop. As I left, I severely damaged my own heart. I thought of all the bad things that had happened throughout the course of our marriage. I asked, "Why was all this crap happening?, When did I become this empty?, and Why do these things happen to good people?"

I guess that was the basis of everything. I felt no one understood the complexity, the battle just to be a part of something, and the simple fact that I needed to be happy. And last but not least, nice guys always seem to finish last.

Chapter Fourteen

It's not a question

but a lesson learned in time

The more that I go on and the more I understand the way this screwy world works, some things are still unbelievable to me. Everyone's perception of a hardship in their life is always different from another. That's the way it is unique. There are two truths in life that are constant for me. It's sad that the world persecutes itself so that these two things remain.

1. Nice guys always finish last.

2. People cause their own afflictions.

These are the two that I believe will be around indefinitely. I say this because it happens every day. You hear about it through the whispers and conversations. I am not saying that I myself am immune to those two facts. It's human nature that we persecute ourselves and others involuntarily.

I am lead to believe therein that nice guys finish last. I will admit that to the fullest. I was made to believe that. It's a truth mainly in business. It seems that the truthful, hard workers of the industry will constantly be shoved under the bus to be run over by the upper class. Raises and promotions are given to undeserving people every day. While we stand unrecognized and under paid questioning the fact of why the asshole still works for the company. Retail is the worst environment in which they try so hard to prove that they are not. Nice people will continue to be the bystanders that get stuck in dead end jobs. I did it for years...I know.

I think it all comes down to personality traits. Good hearted people, the B and C personalities, aren't fit to work within the hate filled, fast paced retail environments. The funny thing is that retail strives upon the hiring of the good natured. The most important aspect of retail sales is customer service. Without the underpaid cashier that greets you upon entering the store or without the helpful beauty assistant the store would be lost. Think about this the next time you go to the store. Try to point out the good people from the fake.

In love, we fail most times. So many times the loves of our lives fall out of reach. Sometimes we get lucky. This even goes back as far as high school. Movies have been made about it. It is awesome to see the big shot lose and the loser win. Both sexes play these foolish games with each other. We hardly ever get anywhere with them.

Take me for example. I spent many years trying to understand the opposite sex. All my good friends were female. I understood more of them than I do my own gender. They say I fell short in love due to I was trying too hard and loving to long. That may be a contradiction of sorts. We all grow up wanting someone to try too hard and love us forever. I was the guy that wanted to prove that I was going to be the greatest fan of your life. I was... captivated by women. I was a crying shoulder to ease the pain and the one that hung from your every word. But like all great tragedies, I was left to many times in the wake of undying love. I was a love addiction and a love suicide. I was engaged four to almost five times throughout my life. I was always the person to be broke up with.

I hear women talk about the perfect man and men do the same when talking of women. Emails are sent through the net describing what we do for each other and what we would like in a partner. I'll put it to you in a way that is easy for me to explain. Nice people are a hard find. There are always going to be bitches and assholes. We have made each other that way for centuries. It's always been the case of once bitten, twice shy. A person can only take so much. A disgruntled man or woman will always show that they have been hurt before. No one wants to have the same hurt over and over again.

I think the point is that we should be careful of the ones we hurt. Nice guys will always think they finish last. The test is to keep fighting to be a nice in a world full of hurt.

We often cause our own afflictions. You often don't even feel the pain. We tend to play the victim far too often. I do it. You do it. We all do it. Our privation of experience is our downfall. We always regret the bad decisions we make. Some people say they don't regret anything (that also being a contradiction.) They say you shouldn't regret things for at one time whatever it was is exactly what you wanted at the time. At any given time, everyone regrets. If even for a brief second, a day, or a week, you regret it when it happens and falters your perceptions. People are far too wrapped up in feeling sorry for themselves'. A lot of people think that the world is persecuting them. I'm sorry, there's a high chance that it just doesn't happen that way. Not many people have the goal to ruin your life. You are in control of whom and what enters your life.

I know that many people don't have the same views as I do. This is where I am at now. I say things like "Nice guys finish last." I believe that life for me has gone this way. I don't live it out through everything I do. I try not to.

Chapter Fifteen

I'll keep your

memory vague

Misty, then, was my answer to a lot of my life's trials. I will give her credit for that. I loved her the only way I knew how. I was content in the way of the relationship. It was the communication meltdown in the end that made me seek the change I needed. I was headed down a one way street the wrong way really fast. I don't think she ever truly understood. I could not get anyone to see the fact that I wanted to control this malfunction. I had lost the ability to make myself happy and caused everyone to feel it just as bad. I had lost the fight that I wanted to fight but I was too weak.

When I left that night, I felt I didn't really know where to go. I had to leave a house that held a lot of precious things and felt I had nothing. I had family and friends, but who was there for the person that was there for everyone else? Even though I didn't like my step-father at the time, I moved in with mom. I hid a lot of the hurt that I was going through that night. I didn't feel the need to show how defenseless I really was.

Two calls were made that night. One was to my mother and the other was to a friend named Jennifer. Jen and I had been talking for a while just as friends. She was the only one I could talk to at the time. We had come from very similar backgrounds. Our lives were generally both riddled with the obscurities of bad timing. I felt she understood a lot of things Misty did not due to those similarities. Whether it was right or wrong at time was still subject of criticism. I just wanted to be comforted by someone that wasn't family. Seems to be a little bit of history repeating don't you think? Jen was becoming another bright light that came to comfort me.

At the time, my heart had taken a lot of erosion due to the river of emotions dealt out over the years. Jen and I met through another friend. I had known her for about four years. She used to visit me when I worked in a photo lab. She had moved away for a while but then moved back around the time Misty and I were having serious issues. Jen was this cute, blue-eyed, red headed woman that always had something to say. She called me from our friends' phone one night and we talked. What happened next was a surprise. She came into my work late that night. For the first time, I was shocked to see her there.

Jen was seven years younger than me. They say that age doesn't matter if you truly love one another. I say, it makes no difference once you are past a certain age. I started dating Jen about two weeks after I left. I know that looks bad. I was still married but dating. With me, you either have me or had me. Misty told me to leave and I considered that the end. Within several months, Misty and I were divorced. I loved her and the girls but with everything that was said and everything I had to endure, I was injured. I didn't want to suffer again.

Jen was wonderful in understanding that I was coming out of a marriage. We took care of each other. I felt special again. I showed her everyday that I could take her heart and care for it. It was something that I had done all my life. I took care of the ones I loved. Now, if I was taking care of me is yet another story. She caught me falling and in turn I fell for her.

I wanted to do everything she did. I needed to be around a person that kept me busy. Again, I had known her for four years prior to our relationship. It wasn't like I barely knew this woman. My thinking was nothing was going to bruise this relationship. We had a lot of things in common verses me and Misty in which we were night and day.

Five months later, Misty and I got a divorce. I truly thought that this was where I wanted to be. I missed Misty, the girls, and the life I had shared with them. It was time to move forward.

I was in complete awe of Jennifer. I loved the way she said certain things, the way she thought that certain things I did was cute, and the way she was passionate about so many things. I treated her like she was a goddess. I tried to give her anything that she needed to feel safe with me. I wanted this relationship to be better than any ones before it. I felt at the time that I would never be hurt by her as much as I hurt before. With her, I was simply left breathless.

I wanted our relationship to be absolutely wonderful. I felt that I was truly being understood. We spent so many times talking that if we had a problem with each other, we would talk it out. We wanted the relationship to go as smooth as possible. They say that if you greatly love something, you surround yourself with it. I wanted to trust her with everything sacred. I just wanted her to know who I was. We spent ten wonderful months together. I really thought she was going to stay. It's hard when you are stuck up on that shelf. That place where you never see the change that is coming.

The rush of feelings I had for her was too much. She couldn't express the same love for me. I wanted her to be in that same place I was. I had this great idea of how I needed to be loved and she wasn't ready to open that portion of her heart. She was still too young. I had handed her a heart truly worth breaking. Some of those pieces will never be put back into the right place.

Chapter Sixteen

No one sings
like you anymore

Denial was my best friend throughout the break-up. I say that in good stride. Jen had made a place inside my tender heart and now I had to live with the fact that I was alone once more. I really took it bad. It was the worst that I have ever taken a break up. You only hear about love stricken melt downs as bad as I was. I guess it came from the suppression of emotions throughout both relationships. I never really dealt or came to terms with the fact of Misty telling me to leave. The way I looked at it was that two women, both I love nonetheless for different reasons, told me to leave. You got to realize that this was supposed to be the end of my story. I didn't want to go on to even more chapters of this book than necessary. I had to put much risk into this thing called happily ever after.

The point was that she needed her freedom. On the other hand, she was the one I ran to in order to get away. But, who could blame her? She still had her young adult life to live. She wanted to pursue her dreams, whatever they were or what might come along. I don't blame her as much as I blame myself. I really should have known what I was getting myself into from the beginning. I should have said what I wanted from the start. Maybe the fork in the road could have been diverted.

I tried everything in my power to find out why this had to happen and why did she not feel the same as me on the basis of love. Many tears were given to something I got my hopes up for. The more I tried to talk to her, the more I got no place at all. She had already made up her mind. She needed her space. I just needed to be in her life but constantly was left out in the cold.

After the realization that she wasn't going to come back, I wanted to hate her. I wanted her to feel sorry for ever leaving and I was mad for ever falling for her. I wanted her to relate the saddest songs to our love. I wanted her to miss me so bad it hurt and I wanted her to think of how bad she had torn my heart from my chest. I tried so hard. This is where I fail myself. I am to forgiving. I couldn't hate her. Even though people were telling me awful shit about her right and left, I refused to listen. I didn't care. I wanted to keep on loving her because she is the one that pushed me to change things inside myself. I was happier when I was with her.

Taking for granted that my father raised me to be loyal and respectable towards women, people have said that I treated Jen to good. I was in love. I treated her the way a woman should be treated. I wanted the world to know that she was truly special to me. It made a difference that I had already been married, I had kids, and I had lived the life of the married man. Our relationship was a win/lose for me. I shared so much of myself with her and she refused to let me know who she was. I am not saying that she didn't try. I think it was that I was trying too hard to get her to do so.

I had fought so hard for the relationship that wasn't meant to happen. I hold nothing against her....well maybe a little a little more than I will admit. I fought for the friendship just as hard. That's something I never wanted to do before. Way back when, with other people in different times, I could care less if I was friends with an ex-lover. I still love her greatly but time has that certain way to ease pain. I feel bad that we weren't meant to be together. I still don't really know how to feel some times. I know that she tried to open up as much as she could just to give me the stability I so desperately needed.

Maybe someday she'll think of me the way I used to be. I believe she has already passed the time of severing any of those feelings. She has become just another spot of light in my once upon a time black tunnel. There will never be a Jen and me. She has become the biggest regret of all. I moved on.

Chapter Seventeen

Take me as I come

because I can't stay long

Throughout my life, I have persevered. I wouldn't be the man I am today without the staggering road I had to walk for so many years. I'll admit that I have grown up too fast. Not many of us stay young as long as we need to. I literally worried my life away as a child. Now was the time for change. Change was my new light.

So, without the added stress of maintaining a relationship, I decided to reflect on why things can't stay constant. I needed to work on a lot of things. I needed to set goals, get back on track with old friends, get to know my father, and find the things that made me happy. (Things other than making others happy before myself).

I had to change because for so long I hated the concept of it. It was my one and only vice. I had already taken the medication route a few years back when I was with Misty and long before I figured out that there was no cure in it. I think I could not be another person willed to take a form of pill just to be content with myself. Sure I had a lot of depersonalization issues, but I was determined. I caught a lot of people off guard when I decided not to be so much a kid any longer. I guess no one expected it at the time. The conception at the time was that Kerry was the one you had to talk sweet words to, the drama induced version of a man compared to a whiney teenager, and the emotional downfallen that at times you had to ignore because no one needed that headache. I never had a will power so to speak on any other issue. Lord knows I should have on some things.

Although the depression in me never truly goes away, it has greatly diminished throughout this time of self improvement though. I still have emotional outburst tendencies and it's hard for me to see things beyond my reasoning sometimes, but I am happier now than ever before. It was really hard for people to believe that in time I would be able to conquer it, to get over that hump, and to eventually stop relying on those spots of light to change me.

Within me, it was all a state of mind. If I got upset that no one ever called to check up on me like I did them, there was no reason to call anymore. At the age of twenty eight, I finally found the peace of mind I needed. My happiness comes from making others happy and from others around me being happy. It has always been that way. I have had enough negativity in my life.

I had put myself out there for people for so long that I was tired of being dragged in the mud. The weight of others people's problems was heavy. But that's how I felt needed. Yet, I stress the issue of causing my own frustrations.

The best thing for me at the time was the love of family and more importantly friends. I have to give great thanks to them. Yet, the strength inside to feel the happiness I deserved was my greatest stride.

I've lost several friends. It's sad to find out about the ones that don't care about you. I actually cared more for one of those friends and I did want her love also. After all was said and done, she infused this rage that lay dormant for so many years. The same rage that I tried to hide from so many. She threw our friendship away. My reactions to her mistrust lead to the ending of two other friendships. I had to do what was better for me. I regretfully bowed out of all trying to sever what I thought we had as far as friendships.

As soon as I figured out that I couldn't be there for the ones that didn't reciprocate the same feelings, I started feeling better. Everything started to turn around. My relationship with my father got closer. Thank God that happened when it did. What made us different was the fact that we were the same but didn't know how to tell each other.

I don't know who said or wrote it but I would love to give credit to the one that said, "I am strong because I am weak, I am beautiful because I know my flaws, I am a lover because I am a fighter, I am fearless because I have been afraid, I am wise because I know I have been foolish....and I can LAUGH because I have known sadness." That, my friend is a good close to this chapter.

Chapter Eighteen

Just a chance that maybe
we'll find better days

I have spent the better part of my life trying to figure this thing called an illness and put it into a category so that it makes sense to not only myself, but to everyone. Depression is different for different people at various ages. It can be as complex as any other major illness. That's why there is so much research done on the subject. And the more the world stresses, the worse it gets.

No one in this world is immune to the fact of depression. No amount of strength, perseverance, or strong mental stability can keep you from feeling sadness. I cannot speak for what everyone else feels at certain times. I can only tell you what I have experienced on a personal basis. Of course, just like any other situation in life, you learn to sympathize with the ones of common mind sets. They always say whatever doesn't kill you only makes you stronger.

Jen, without knowing it, destroyed the idea of what a wonderful thing I thought love was. Instead of finding a path to what I needed, I found a detour and then a road block. If she would have been completely honest with me in the beginning, then the disaster could have been avoided. I finally got to a point where I just didn't give a damn what she thought of what her fault was in our former relationship. Even being just a friend was just tiring. I was exhausted. I was tired of playing the foolish games. She was leaving way before the relationship was over. I guess, the point being, is that sometimes we must push ourselves to move on. (Whether if it hurts us more or not.) When it comes to relationships and marriage, some people were never meant to look good on paper.

It's all a part of relinquishing all the bad memories. You have to baptize your emotions so to speak. We get stuck in this rut of self pity that even you yourself do not appreciate. No one likes the person that always plays the pity me card. The minute you decide to stop feeling so damn bad for yourself is when you begin to strengthen. There's a darkness inside us all that prevents us from moving forward. It's so easy to think negative in life. Finding the light becomes harder and harder the more you do nothing about it. Self preservation at this point needs to create your emotional states' longevity. The longer you sit around in your darkness, the less apparent in reality your happiness becomes.

I can't say I performed this rescue from the depths of my so called black tunnel all by myself. I will admit that all the small things truly bothered me. The help was there when I needed it whether I wanted it or not. More often I refused it. I refused a lot of people that were just trying to help. I have seen the errors of what I didn't do. I didn't do a lot of things along the way. Things such as possibly could've helped in a way of leading me to emotional salvation. Truth be known, that people tend to care if you let them. My family and friends were there all along but I refused to let them in. My thoughts were that I didn't want my family to worry about me. This was for me to burden not for others to burden for me.

It's this thing called hindsight that kicks us in the ass. It's all a fact of life. If we didn't have it, we would never learn. This is why I say that more often than not that we cause our own afflictions. I know I've had my fair share of looking back. It's funny how that part of reality kicks in. It is funny how in control of yourself you think you are and how unaware you become to the fact that someone actually cares. I don't need to contradict myself at this point. I did have help towards the road of happiness, but I didn't need medication to do so. It was all a mind set. I had a goal and I wanted it so bad that it hurt. It all relates back to fear. The fear of change had a nasty grasp for a very long time. The fear of never becoming the person I was meant to be was a big issue. The fear of becoming a different subdued person on medication was a bigger one.

It's crazy to think about how much love and hurt affects us all. To consider ourselves alive we must obtain love and endure hurt. I want to explain that most times, Love and Hurt are partners. We cause so much others pain in order to be happy. We shy away from so many things in life in order to prevent our self and others to not be so much heartbroken. Many are unwilling to take a chance on a sure thing simply because the world has created an unrealistic risk upon everything.

So many times we hear stories about how we should have done things in life. It's this regret that haunts us continually. The ghosts of these things we have rightfully named Coulda, Shoulda, and Woulda tend to remain in our hind sight.

It's been on my mind a lot lately. I hate the fact that we persecute others for the past we have left. I have felt that I have had to pay for every hurtful word every former lover has stricken across my heart. How did it ever get to this acquisition? It's so far gone now. Isn't a true love supposed to bind us? Never should it feel like a struggle just to tell others we love them.

This chapter eluded me for quite some time. It seemed like forever to say the least. I wanted to convey the importance of a mind set. Although positive or negative thoughts may lead you, everyone has the will power or determination to fix our own perspectives. Every choice we make is ours and ours alone. It's kind of like the concept of quitting the smoking habit cold turkey. With everything negative throughout the span of my depression, I kept confident with the idea that there was going to be a happier place. A place where I fit in. A place where I was the hero of my story. I was truly done with all the aspects of being sad. I was tired of having paper thin defenses and trying to grin and bare it at every turn where I felt threatened. I felt I needed to rid myself of my shots of emotional pain. I truly needed to be baptized. Vindicated.

Moving past a lot of the pain and letting the hurt subside wasn't easy. You get to where you have to do something. You can only take so much before you snap. Friends and family tend to do a balancing act. If you don't have the support of one, you rely on the other. I felt throughout my childhood that I wasn't the exact fit within my family, so my friends were more important in my world. That is, what little amount of friends I did have. My friends made me feel like I was needed. Even then, having all female friends while looking for some understanding wasn't a bright idea but I sustained.

The point is that your family is bias in the way of your feelings. They know which buttons to push and try not to hurt your feelings most of the time. I believe that's what is missing from a lot of families is simply positive interaction and reinforcement. Your friends depend upon your strengths. My strength was a sense of humor.

My weaknesses far outweighed my one and only positive that I knew I had. I say just one because my other passion in life was art and when you're in your teens it really doesn't bring as much joy as laughter. After all, laughter is the best medicine. When I think back, I wish I had the strength to conquer all the issues a lot earlier. But I was raised to respect others, to fight only when needed, to keep your words sweet in the fear of having to eat them later, and protect your heart from anyone that will leave you crushed. That's the way I saw it. Needless to say, I loved too many. Though their many faults, I still loved with the pieces I had left.

The worst thing was holding in all the rage, the corrupted interjections, and all the intolerable sadness. I became addicted to holding it all in. It's a shame really that you don't understand things until you've experienced them first hand. When everyone told me that holding in all this hurt was eventually going to cause this much torment, I let it slide right off. I was more concerned that people were going to look at me differently if I had that many problems. Like I said, it wasn't anyone else's burden to bear.

The second one was the incapability to open up to anyone. I thought that I was alone and alone I stayed. I really didn't know how to open up as much as I needed to. Hell, most of the time, I didn't know what I was truly upset or emotional about. I know that speaking up about the crazy stuff that upsets us may be one of the hardest things in this world to do. I will attest to it. I never insisted on going against the grain. I single handedly kept myself isolated from the world. You should never cage something you wanted to see fly. I was meant to fly but then again, I always had the fear of falling; of failing. And this is where it all stems from, the fear of failure.

The third one, I guess, is the most vital. Needless to say, I lived for the past. There's a reason I say live for and not live in. I wanted the past to somehow come back. I had become so reliant on my own pain in the effort to help others that I tended to stay there with it. I was addicted to something even more harmful in an effort to decrease pain.

Helen Keller was quoted in saying, "When one door of happiness closes, another opens; but often we look so long at the closed door that we do not see the one which has opened for us."

The truth is that I despised other people that always blamed their past for the irrationalities in their lives. Secretly I hated the one thing that was a major part of who I was. I hated it because I knew that it was a part of me that I wasn't ready to change.

No matter how many good days I could have, I was always going to go home feeling not quite myself. I believe that the saddest people in the world are the ones that'll try to convince you that there is nothing wrong more often. Maybe, that's why clowns are creepy.

As I've said, the study of depression is a long lasting one. My belief that depression can only be subdued or suppressed is justified for me. My mind just works that way. God gave us the gift of memories to learn from our faults in hopes of not doing them again. It's not here for you to use as an excuse to fall on black days. The hardest part isn't finding who we want to be, it's being content in the fact of who we need to be.

It's up to you what you want to keep or bring to your life. You can't let this broken heart disease called depression destroy you.

Chapter Nineteen

You can go

You can start all over again

You know the part of the dream when you realize that it is in fact only a dream? Better yet, the relief you feel when you wake up to find the nightmare isn't real? I know that feeling. There is really nothing you can do when you believe what you see is real. As you can see, I try to explain certain things so that I can relate to you on some sort of common ground.

There's a reason why this chapter is titled as such. We all change like the seasons. Most of us hate the fact of change. Starting over is scary. Some of these seasons we face are longer than others. We all like to think we are living the dream but sometimes we wake up to find that what we see for ourselves is the nightmare. I had to wake up from a dream. I had to learn that my season of hurt needed to end. The past is what I got to let go. As hard as that is sometimes, I have too. The hardest lesson to learn is to let go. I want to believe in myself. I want to be someone who believes. I believe that love will keep us alive.

I started writing with the belief that I was going to be happier. I poured my heart and soul into something I believed that in fact could be a reality. I want to say "I did this!"

Soon after my world had crashed, I decided to move on. I realize that sentence was typed faster than it took to actually move on. I needed to be comfortable again. I lived with my mother at the time, so I could not just leave and go about my single life. Single life does not suite me in the least. It took some time to find a path. Along the way I lost a new car and had to make many sacrifices, but I made it through. I also found a love I had known for years but never felt.

With this being the turning point of this book, I really want to tell you that everything in the world is trying to be aligned once again. I now found myself, I found my family, and I found something that I forever needed. Misty and I began to talk again. I found a new love that I never knew I had, the love for myself. It took me so many wasted years to realize that everyone loves to hear that you love them, but more so, they love to feel it. I loved to feel needed.

As for Misty and I, we were together for another year and a half. It took us that long to figure that we weren't meant to be. We never got remarried within that time and I guess it was fate that we hadn't. It was hard for me to love her for the woman she was and even harder for her to accept it. After living in the same house and feeling like I was the babysitter, I decided to move out after six months. That's way longer than anyone could have imagined me staying in a house where I didn't feel quite as loved as before. It was me just being stubborn in a way.

It took some time to sort out feelings and the adjustment to being single really suddenly in my life, but it was my choice. I could have stayed and fought for her but truly, I saw it going the exact same way it always went. I love her and there was no doubt of that but not the same way as I did. This was the only way I was going to be happy and carry on.

I had to find that one person that'll be truly happy with me.....myself.

Everyone deserves to be happy. I once had a dark tunnel. It's a little bit different now. I turned a lot of those spots of lights into beacons that defeated some of that darkness.

There is one thing I have learned for sure and it's that it seems that only in dreams and in love that are we vulnerable, yet we depend on both in order to feel alive.

Chapter Twenty

Love will keep

us alive

I am a truly compassionate person. That's who I am. I grew up relatively misunderstanding the basis of why I cared so immensely for everything and everyone. I became sympathetic at every turn for most of my young life.

But now I know. I love to be this way. I have found that it connects me with so many people on so many levels. Also, within this realization, I wanted to connect my writings with other compassionate people.

This is my testament of how I truly view the nature of the world around me. It's just me, sharing how my heart reacts when it comes to friendship and love, in family and fortune, and how to survive being a loving spirit in life.

Without being told, anyone can see that even with my imperfections of being happy, with depression or figuring out exactly who I was, I have been stubborn in loving others the way I felt they needed to be loved. At times, that's really a harder concept than most. Not every person tries to understand such different levels in which someone can love them. I love, have loved, and will continue to love a great many of others within my crazy, little aspect of a life. It's crazy to think about how I think of this continual need sometimes. I tend to hear a lot of negative things throughout the course of my daily life but that doesn't deter me in thinking that tomorrow is a newer day. I look for a tomorrow that doesn't hold the stresses and the issues of today or even the day after the next day's tomorrows.

In a way, love has kept me alive. I say that because it has been an unwavering fact for some time now. Times when even I thought I was without love, it was there. The compassionate nature and love of others has given me hope all my life. And, I'm trying to not make that sound too corny or as a fake inspiration. My compassion has always been there. It has showed me things I'd never imagined. There are truly some loving hearts in this world.

Everyone hopes to see a positive change in life with every waking moment. We share videos from day to day where kindness and generosity is shared and given. Kindness has become such a rare trait these days that we are in shock, and in awe of it, when we see it. It has become more shocking to see a person rescuing animals, giving the homeless food, or granting a wish of the kindred spirit of a dying child. You wouldn't think that such things would be considered rare but they are. Rare...,this idea...,this love of another.

But here is the statement that I must add. Being compassionate, having a caring soul towards others, and putting everything aside for one moment just to let someone or something feel that you are concerned for them really adds to life itself.

It's all a part of loving thy neighbor. The most respected, recognized, and sometimes possibly the most hated thing in the world is love. Love is the only thing in the human mind-set that can utterly destroy you at one glance and still, you crave it again and again.

It's been attributed to saving the human race. "For God so <u>loved</u> the world, that he gave his only begotten Son, so that whosoever believeth in him should not perish, but have everlasting life." – John 3:16

Is there such power in that word, the word "love"? Is it because we fear it? Do we fear it every time we admit to having it or even feeling it? Does it invoke this sense of disillusion? It does, doesn't it? Are we so afraid to let people feel this way towards us? I will tell you that most of us are. Telling others that we love them is not easy. We all want to be loved in returned- to be, at least, told that we are as much a part of someone's heart as they are ours. Maybe love comes with too many conditions now. So why do we do it continuously? Love is just like death to us, full of unknowns and uncertainties.

It's amazing that such tiny things in our lives are of the greatest significance. I will admit that I am guilty of loving too long and too often. Is that so bad, loving more than most? I look at it as the compassionate side of things. Sure it skews my emotions sometimes but not one person in my life will ever doubt that I care for them. It's true and it's honest. That's pretty much a driving force. It's not an easy task of putting ourselves out there. It puts us in a place that puts others before ourselves. It's a trait that pushes me to be a care giver more often than I like to be but I react to it as a normalcy. It creates a state of vulnerability and that's a place you may have feared for as long as you remember. Rejection is a defeating aspect. Everyone hates that feeling. We have made a world where we are afraid to share loving words for we have made it out to look as if it is a weakness. I refuse to let this be a subject of introversion. Having a love for others needs to be strong; boastful in its existence.

Love is love. It doesn't matter who you love. The important thing to remember is that you have the ability to love and to learn from loving.

This is what sets us apart. Being compassionate isn't easy. Maybe compassionate people will agree with me. Saying "I love you" to everyone whom you feel needs to hear it is complex. It's complex because of the many conditions love has. I feel it has to be. I do feel it is needed though. It's cumbersome to be positive to others who do not feel they need it or when it's too hard for them to hear. It is a hurtful realization. Not everyone can accept these words because, like I said, they fear them. Love is truly a misused term for us. We say we love a lot of things, but do we? Do you think we say it because we almost expect to hear or feel it back? That's the point, we like to hear it. We like to know we are cared for.

I knew this girl at one time. I truly do not know her any longer. She had a problem with self worth. She really felt she was unloved so she never found the love she needed. It seemed she feared it. Her fear that this love was not reciprocated left her a little uncomforted; a little empty. She felt her love was never heard or felt. Purely, it was the ghost she could never set free. Knowing this, she had no desire to change it. Being afraid to say anything for fear of losing the relationship as she knew it was something of a crutch.

The content of what you're trying to obtain never changes if you never tend to it to make it better for yourself. I always referred to it as my version of "never stirring the pot". You want something to change? You must stir the pot. And it might be painstaking at first and possibly stressful to an end. It might open some old wounds. It might also open some people's eyes; maybe even their minds. In this case, of the aforementioned person from above, she felt her mother never showed her the love she craved. She was often wondering and quietly questioning the love her mother was unable to show. And how was her mother to know how she felt? She never gave her mother any indicators that this had upset her for years.

This is why we should let our emotions be known. We all know what our version of love is. Defining our version of it is often difficult. We all have different definitions for it but we know nonetheless. We are all born into sin. We are born into selfishness and into hate. We are born because of love. We are all born knowing how to love. We will always have to work on love more than hate. Hate is and will always be something of a learned emotion but I can say, love will treat you far better than hatred ever will.

This is where a compassionate person stays true to his causes. We fight for understanding and we strive for communication. We stir the pot. We fight for better understanding of others every day. We learn to not only listen but to observe. Sometimes it's what people aren't saying that we need to hear. I believe that, without compassion in our hearts, we are living a life in poverty.

We live our lives to be loved. Love keeps us alive because we live for it. Love could be considered the only thing we can take with us when we die.

Chapter Twenty-One

Standing All Alone
Against The World Outside

Without a doubt, compassion and depression are always at bad terms with one another. Compassionate people with depression are viewed as negative opportunists. Sure, the world presents a lot of negativity to us and we endure it for the simple fact of finding a speck of compassion. Even though we have seen the worst or experienced the hardest times, we still believe that there is some good out there somewhere. This very well may be a double-edged sword scenario at its best. We are a lost breed, I've give you that.

As a compassionate person, I grew up with one of the lowest self esteems. I never wanted it to be that way. I hid this fact forever in my youth. I loved for people to see me happy. I was addicted to the fact that I wanted people to see me happy. I felt I lived in everyone's shadow. I hated it but I knew my place or at least where I thought my place was. This is how I was standing alone; outside looking in. I lived on the edge of my little brother's shadow. It wasn't his fault. It never was. Even my friends would tell me that my brother was more attractive than I was. They never knew how it broke down my emotional wall that was so ill constructed at the time. There were times that I simply wasn't chosen. Time after time after time I was not the one that people were interested in. I never knew what was wrong. I tried to fathom where I was unattractive or unwanted. What could have I had done to be put in that place? It's just one of the things that bothered me in my youth.

I was an outcast in my mind and social standing. I had so many friends that were female but hardly had a girlfriend or anyone interested in me until I was well into my teenage years. I know that sounds weird but I was truly compassionate towards many people, I wanted to be a part of many lives. I wanted to be near people so I was there for them as a friend; always wanting to be more. It wasn't until my life as a young adult did people start coming forward and telling me that I was an object of their affection as well but they never told me. Well, it was too late now. Our lives had surpassed our imaginations. It wasn't the same as it was when we were innocent. Being a compassionate person has always had its heartaches. Trust me, it was a long journey; a journey I never quite realized I was on until I was around twenty-seven years old or so. I lost a good many friends, or should I say future love interests, due to the fact of never quite getting that my compassionate nature was a two-way street.

It's never the case of simply changing the way we think and feel. I did try to be tougher and more uncaring but I couldn't sustain it. It's intertwined within our hearts. We are raised this way. I never knew it was this way. I grew up thinking that you could choose how your emotions were controlled. The truth is, if you are compassionate at heart, then your heart will be tender thusly for the livelihood of others. In order to cure others, we must sacrifice a little piece of ourselves, saddening our hearts to make others feel loved. It's an acceptance of being strong for others before yourself, even though it may make us hide our own true feelings. It tends to stay the same unless you break it. By breaking it down or having someone taking it away from you, we become the victim. It's sad but true, but this is how it portrays itself in the end. But....there's this strength that stays hidden. It tells you that you are far from being a victim. That you are stronger for it. No matter how much you destroy it, no matter how hard someone beats it out of you; you still find it. It's just a notion of a greater truth. Light somehow defeats darkness, every single time.

No matter, how many people bullied me when I was in grade school, no matter how many times a person rejected my friendship, and no matter how many times I wasn't the one the girl picked, I rose up and stood for it once again. Why? Because I always thought that it would eventually get better. I just beat myself up emotionally so badly and yet with every positive thing in my life I became more vigilant in the fact of brighter days. This is why depression is so widespread throughout with compassionate people. Some of us figure that it's easier to live with our own negativity than to share it with others. We don't want to burden others with our issues but on the same accord, we are happy to listen to yours. Depression, moreover, is expressed as a ghost. Many do not believe it is there. Some see it but simply choose to ignore its existence therefore pushing it away from them. And then there are the ones that believe it haunts them every single day. Our own negativity becomes our ghost. It lingers. It hides in the recesses of our selves. It just lives there, temporarily suspended; waiting for you to come to terms with its validity. It's not until we get fed up and defeated do we try to rid ourselves of this negativity in our lives. From the outside looking in, we always tend to ask why we keep the negative parts within our lives. Maybe it's a part of us.

Chapter Twenty-Two

You're The Meaning In My Life

You're The Inspiration

When I was young, my dad collected this comic strip called "Love is..." They still publish it to this day in some papers. He had hundreds of these one-panel, simply drawn cartoons. This is possibly where my first idea of what love was came from. I loved reading these because dad loved to collect them. It also told me a little about him. So, I have made this poem from that memory.

LOVE IS...

...something untouchable. To be felt and not to see.

...something shared between you and me.

...unrealistic in the way we care for one another.

...rainy days and staying warm with each other.

...the intangible feeling that we'll always be together.

...sharing thoughts to communicate better.

...saying "I love you" when times seem hard.

...saying it all with just a little card.

...trying hard to be sweet and harder to be naughty.

...a perfect blend of mind and body.

I have written love poems all my life. When I started writing anything, it was poetry. As a matter of fact, the first piece I ever wrote was simply called "Love". I was in fourth grade and I kind of shocked my teacher that I didn't chose to write about something more "child-like". It seems love is something I was in awe about then and even now to this day.

So...chapter twenty-two...what should I write? Where should I go with this? I've had an idea, an idea that has been with me for some time. It's just a simple idea really. I have loved a great many people throughout my life. I say this because it's been a challenge at times but I always found a different degree of love for others. I rarely ever found a person I didn't like. That either puts me in a place of wealth or a place of just being naive. Whether it be one or the other, I feel comfortable in my standing. To conclude on the topic of this chapter, I have chosen to write a big love letter. A letter to all the ones I have loved.

To all the ones I have loved,

Just know that at one time in my life I had a love for you and probably still do. I still think of you time to time. I will always be continually compassionate and caring towards you. And even to those that I do not talk to any longer or ever see, know that I still find a way to remember you. To everyone in my life, I hope this helps you understand how I loved you this long.

To the girl in I chased in 4th grade- You will always be the first I admired.

To the girl that made me cry in middle school- Thanks for being so understanding.

To the girl that went out with the preacher's son- What a beautiful woman you have become.

To the fiery girl on the apartment playground- I miss the times when we were young. I will always love you. We met each other at eleven and never quite lost each other.

To the cute one I flirted with on the bus- You and your sisters will always hold strong within my heart. You are truly beautiful, inside and out.

To the lost one that couldn't be happy and never found me- Too bad you took the low road.

To the one with hope that wore my ring around her neck- So glad you have the life that has made you happy. Sorry I broke your heart...I really didn't mean to.

To the beautiful popular girl that I lucked into having in my life- I embarrassed myself in her presence time after time because I liked her. :)

To the tom-boy that watched X-files- You will always be my partner in crime.

To one of my first East Texas crushes (although she never knew and I have never mentioned) that always made me feel comfortable- Her smile and hugs are always the best.

To the girl that was too young- I miss you. Make the angels smile.

To the blonde that spent the night- I see you finally got your life turned around. I believed in you. Too bad friendship never worked for us either.

To the friend that was a lot like me- God bless you brother. There were so many good times had.

To my friend, my brother that loves comedy and comics- Wolverine is always going to be the best.

To the woman that had my child- I did love you once but it was you that changed. Thank you for a beautiful daughter.

To the reluctant red-head- Thanks for the time we had. Too bad we let others ruin our friendship.

To the cute woman that wanted to find the passion again- I'm glad you found a smile. I love your smile and great heart.

To the one that got too confident too fast- Too bad you never saw what I saw.

To my beer drinking, partying brother in Oklahoma- Damn, I miss you brother. Love you man. You are always family to me.

To the soldier that loves cigars- Thanks for the friendship..well..and all the great damn cigars back in the day.

To my friends that are family because of our loving friendships- There's a world of love for you. You have been a part of my family all my adult life. Family isn't always related but I will always choose you as part of mine.

To my family...my honest to God family- You are my soul; so glad to be a part of your lives.

To the girl...umm hmm...teenager/semi-grown little woman that's my daughter- I know life is hard but I will forever try to be a part of yours. Love you so much.

To the curly-headed, brown-eyed Canadian I chose to be my better half- Thank you for loving me completely... goofiness and all.

Once again, what I have here is another chapter that was more thought provoking to write the more I thought about it. Moreover, the past is painful when you look back and think of all the time you have hurt or even hurt others for what you thought would be your happiness in the end. But, it's good to write...to remember where you have been and what you have overcome. Love and compassion can be both a little weird at times. At this moment in time, I will continue to love and care for these people who have been here throughout my life. It's a love I thought I would lose somehow. So glad I kept it.

Chapter Twenty-Three

And All Of My Flaws
Are Laid Out One By One

I have lived with all my many flaws, my ghosts if you will, for as long as I can remember. It seems it is harder to forget a great many things throughout my life. I think as a tender-hearted person and a compassionate soul it's difficult not to be haunted. Maybe it's the fact that I hate change. I accept it but I do not like it. I tend to go through this period of great acceptance trying to sustain my heart when I see it as a weakness. Haunted by what some may call regret. Maybe it's my way of bullet proofing my idea of what I have become.

Spending a life protecting what I am truly passionate about is ideally the hardest work I have ever done. I was strong for others when I found it hard to be strong for myself. I will forever try to save another even if that means I fall apart. The difference is that I am good at the rebuilding of my newer self. I will not let a single change of weather destroy a season.

In choosing to wake up every day as a compassionate heart, it has had its challenges, but it's been this way forever. It has gotten me through some of what I thought was the most tragic and depression-based portions of life.

Believe or not, as I have always said, my childhood was spent trying to be loving towards others and simply dying for acceptance. As a heartbroken kid I tried my best to hide so much pain and I never knew where it came from. I tried to fit in at school...and I did to the best of my ability. I was engineered from the beginning to be compassionate to everyone. It put me in a place of indifference where I felt I was different than everyone. And, with that being said, it brings me to something else.

I honestly and truthfully do not remember the year much less the many other minute details that I should remember of that day. I know I was young. I do know that. The place in life when you were still able to go outside and play for recess and it always occurred after lunch so that you weren't falling asleep when you got back to the classroom. It was always the thirty minutes, in its simplicity, that was the very root of having fun and making friends.

Fall had begun its slow course but it was still warm enough to go play without shivering to death. The sun was still at that comfortable amount of warm followed by a light touch of a breeze.

I went to a small, quaint school in North Texas where everyone was knowledgeable of everyone else. It was just a close knit, tiny 2A school at the time as far as sports were concerned. We, as a class, only consisted of about 50 of us. The class was about even in the ratio of boys and girls. It was good.

With me always a being compassionate, loving soul I was always the lover and never the fighter. I did my fair share of latching onto whoever wanted my friendship. I truly never met a stranger. I always found it was so much easier to make friends with the girls of the class. So, they made up a good percentage of my companions. I liked them. I had crushes on a lot of them (all of them). Their friendships completed me in so many ways. It wasn't until I was older that I felt less complacent among my sweet friends.

I had a few guy friends but they were few and far between at the time. It was weird for them to see me in awe of my other friendships.

I was picked on from a young age because being a compassionate male was sort of out of place from everyone else's world. I wanted to share a great love towards everyone.

As time grew on, my friends found me bothersome and in the way with me being the only guy in the friend schematic. So, when kindness met with negativity, I was forced to find camaraderie among others. As weeks persisted, I found it harder to find different friendships. I was left alone to wait out recess by sitting against a wall or walking the length of the yard.

There were a lot of things confined within my small but ever growing, but simple heart. I felt misunderstood and mislead by the reasons my friends gave me as to possibly needing a little space from me from time to time.

One day, while walking the length of the grounds, a group of girls asked me to come and talk to them. Four girls I had practically known since kindergarten age, were insistent in talking to me. I knew their presence in my world and now I had become a presence in theirs. These four girls were the girls everyone liked and everyone looked up to. They were the "popular" girls of our meek little class. I felt as if I was special just to be in the realm of their interest. For within this tiny speck of time, their interest was in fact...me.

I will remember that day for as long as life allows me. They took me aside and said that they had noticed I was alone. They asked if I wanted to hang around them for a while. I don't remember their exact words, but I remember the feeling. They acted as if they had shared one common idea. They told me that they wanted to be my friend. If I ever needed them, just ask.

Deep down, something was awakened. The faith in my humanity and the reassurance of my own humility was restored for what little life had shown thus far. I still get these butterflies, that little yet wonderful feeling inside when I remember back. It remains one of those heartfelt memories I will forever treasure.

Until this day, I haven't had the chance to thank all four, now grown, women for what a wonderful thing they did all so long ago. That it truly made the day of one weird, emotional little boy that thought he was unimportant.

Here is to you Dana Gary, Erin Wilkerson, Emily Owens, and Sherry Kirby. Thanks for the smallest portion of a memory but the biggest gesture I could have received throughout my young life. I hope I get to thank you personally someday, whether you remember this sweet moment or not.

Needless to say, I found my friends as family from then on. Time moves on and on into an unsure future. I'd rather be a brother to all these girls than run the risk of losing them. From then on, I started having a family of sisters. I love my sisters, whether they used to be a love interest or not.

Chapter Twenty-Four

Stuck In The

Middle With You

I have always adhered to the truth that the greatest hurt you can cause to yourself is ultimately caused by you. I think part of it for me is that I got my hopes up too high for the many things that I wished could've happened throughout my life.

But we all have this grand gift of memory. A gift God granted as one of the greatest things that we can possess. It's great how we cherish so many good memories and how we cherish them keeping them within our hearts. Life and love is a base for all these great memories. I only bring this up because of the fact that they play such an important part with us being compassionate for ourselves. I think the good memories keep us moving towards a tranquility of our own.

Being soft-hearted, I find myself in the middle of most things. We find ourselves helplessly caught up in everything within everyone's lives. But it is intuitive for me (for us) to be this way. We continue to be unwavering in the fact that we need to be a part of other's lives. If more people came together...met in the middle...we wouldn't have to face so many adversities throughout our lives; never fearing that we are a dying breed.

In time, I became accustomed to the middle. I stayed in the complicated vortex of my idea of what my happiness's origin was. I habituated in the stagnant place where I felt involved and understood at the very center of my true worth to others. I was happy to be in the middle of friendship arguments, lover's spats, family quarrels, and more often than not, trying to talk to someone else about who they like while pining after them myself. It tends to get convoluted a lot of the times, this being happy by seeing others happy. It becomes a day in the life of the drama induced the further you dig into the whole aspect of it all.

As once stated by the American poet named Marilyn Hacker, "There is something very satisfactory about being in the middle of something." I always liked that quote. It's true. Everyone likes to have some sort of involvement in some way, just to say, "Hey, I was there"..."I helped"... "It was my idea"...

But just like everything in life, there is always a negative whenever a positive is created. Nearly all my life, I was in that place. A place that created happiness while contributing to happiness in others. I felt good about the smiles, the laughter, the hugs, and the positivism of all things in my middle. My middle was comforting a lot of the time but as I got older it became less about my ownership of my middle. When I put myself into that place it was my comfort zone...my happiness. It was when others took advantage of my comforting place and threw me into the middle is when it started to become increasingly cumbersome. The problem was that my negative was used to create a positive. I loved the attention of the middle and when it came to the creation of other's positives, it made me feel as if it wasn't so much of a negative.

I think my middle and my idea of compassion were intrinsically linked. It was natural for me to connect the two. Moving outside the city limits of this middle was something that had to be done. I love to help others. It's a part of me that never gets old (my heart of hearts if you will). But as they say, "There's just no helping some people". I suffered so many burns from walking across fires to save others that I became hesitant to come running when others screamed for help. I was once told that when you get run over by just being yourself, you begin to question the road you are walking. It makes sense. The middle needed to lose its *universality within me. When you're comfortable with this mentality you become used and addicted to this idea of only being needed for others dependability.*

Okay...sorry...I kind of veered off there for a second. With everything in life, routines get old and things need to change every once in a while. *I want to be a part of so many people's lives but not this way. The reciprocation variable just wasn't in my favor with placing myself in the back and forth game of needful things.*

So, after my divorce from my first wife in 2006, I wanted change. No more bullshit and no more excuses from myself or from others. Certainly, no one was going to create my happiness other than myself. This was my touch of reality. Understandably, I regret putting up with so many negatives thinking that it would end up generating a positive for so long. I wanted a change.

There comes a point where everything you hold precious has to be let go. You have to agree with me upon this because even in death we let go. It becomes too damn difficult to keep these things, these habits; these objects, whether tangible or not, that we have become comfortable with. All of our vices; the negativity that we fear, it all has to be set free. It's of all these things that cause you stress within your life. These things like holding on to those ideals that you know are wrong but you maintain. Holding on because you fear that you cannot survive without them. They will kill you. They slowly eat away at the very thought of a happiness you deserve. Thoughts that have become the cigarette you have to have in which to maintain life; causing your body to hurt with its poison. It's our job to say what people, these habits, we let stay within our lives. Sometimes, it's more of a heartache to simply let it go, but in order to survive, we have to. We have to close our eyes, take a breath, and let go.

In 2007, the Kerry that everyone knew or the Kerry that existed within the walls and realm of this particular time line, died. I know that sounds stupid but as soon as change happens, a rebirth; an awakening if you will, happens.

With this being said, I felt as this next thing was needed.

-Kerry R. Jeffrey, lifelong friend to many and free of heart for the most part of a courageous life, died last night due to complications of a tender heart. Jeffrey, age 30 was never before strong willed enough to beat his emotions but in his final days he was awakened and revealed an unknown side of himself yet to his life. The events that lead up to his demise, proved that he was the strongest of us all. He beat his transgressions and became the man everyone knew he could be. Happy.

These past years of clarity have shown me a lot of people's true colors. It has also shown me that I am better than the ones that lie, that manipulate, that will corrupt others, and the ones that proved that they never really loved me.

I will forever be a compassionate, heartfelt human being. I have proved it time and time again. I have given my time, my money, and my heart to others regardless of the fact that I may not have seen anything in return. I have been understanding and caring to an end. Now to the things I am not....

I am not a liar, a manipulator, two-faced, money-hungry or power-driven. I have nothing to gain from these things. When I say I will do things, I will do them. I believe in "Give and then you shall receive." I give my heart and, among all things, respect to all that give it back to me. There are greedy people in this world that thrive on others. Others, unlike you...unlike me. My compassion for others is not a weakness nor should it be for you either. If it is taken into that consideration, my loyalties are steered away from the ones treating me that way. My love has not a monetary value. I will not buy other's hearts to make myself feel love. Money is evil. I will blame many things upon it's scummy worth. Can we survive without it?...No. Can we survive without the love of another?...Maybe but not likely.

Not me in any case. To live without love and money seems subjective but it's a balance. Neither one will prove better than the other. Money doesn't create love nor does love create physical wealth but we die for one or the other.

There cannot and will not be anymore struggle for power when it comes into my life. If people want to be here for me; with me, then be here as I am for you. That's all I ask. These people in my life are here for a reason and everyone here is kept within my heart. They know why I put them there. I am going to keep on loving. It has got me this far.

There's always a beginning, a middle, and an end. In 2007, I began to put an end to a middle. You never have to be put in the middle, so try not to end up there.

I feel as if this rant had to written. Maybe it has taken this long to form those words the way they needed to be written. Change takes time. It's been so many years and it hasn't been without its trials, but I am still naturally compassionate to the end but it's my terms and no one else's.

Chapter Twenty-Five

But If It's Love You're Looking For

Then I Can Give A Little More

When I was in fourth grade, the first time I began to write, I began by writing poetry. I tried writing poetry before I ever knew what poetry was. I loved the way someone could write it with emotion. Even if I didn't understand it, I still read it. I included poetry in the first part of this book so I feel it has to be in the second. I guess with poetry, I loved that I can invoke a feeling without out-right saying it. This is how I learned about how deeply people loved others. So, to catch you up on the poetry that I have written the past couple of years...

Muse

There are only a few things I remember. I catch myself dreaming, lingering with the backfill of emotions whilst they tug at shadows of those heartstrings. Smelling the enticing smell that inherited the pores of her skin and so longed for my attention.

It seemed to be a pattern I traced when I look back upon bittersweet memories of a love that ignited. Just to be a bright reflection inside those eyes...I remember.

Within, a tender song in the tones that bellowed from her whispers. I, loving the warmth of her breath, tingled from the idea of her being close. I remember the sound of my name upon her tongue. And I reflect on the warmth of my heart just to hear her form the word. I loved the way she carried herself, positive and strong, not letting the convictions of life pull her down. She never tried to be beautiful, she just was. She walked slightly resembling a rhythmic dance that took center stage. The shadow displayed on brightest of days was gently poetic to the sun.

Her gentle laugh was caressed from within and hidden behind the simplest of smiles. To be a muse among sinners should have been truly an honor and to her I held most high.

Too Many Times-

There have been too many times that I was sad over too little of things. It was often times I felt unwanted and alone. A tirade of words, here and there, where I felt frustrated by change. Transgressions have come and gone when I knew I was mad at the world. Strange days had passed where all I wanted was sleep. Days went by where all I wanted was for others to fail. Nights crept along; all the while I felt things throughout the lyrics. Daydreaming of poetry, music, laughter and love. Pondering... Too many times where things eventually got better. Where I stood up and knew I got had gotten stronger. When I starting counting the moments instead of minutes. Hours began to be blessings of time; of life. Too many times, I thought this is going to break me. But then again, too many times, I forced a smile and dried a tear. Too many times, I saw a better day.

Ailments-

Her eyes never saw how others used her;

Really never listening or ever knowing.

Her visions were a bit fuzzy; her sight always a blur.

She had an inner ear issue for what they figured.

For everything you told her she believed;

Trusting little words and every tiny whisper.

Her lungs were just too small and breathing labored.

She tended to hold her breathe quite long;

Waiting for love to do her such favors.

Her heart, although healthy, skipped many a beat;

Being left caught in the air with strangers;

After they had swept her off her feet.

She walked a little funny, kind of a loosely steer.

She always walked back to her past;

Her reasons were never stated clear.

She had her ailments thinking she was hexed.

She was going to be better next time.

She's protected again and for what comes next.

Rest-

Then the riots started. It began, on that very day, never thinking a battle could've raged so suddenly. He had lost far too much from within himself to battle any attackers on that morning.

Then... she came along, bravely fighting with a sword of hope. She carefully aimed a gun of truth; of light. She banished all the darkness and all the spies from behind the enemy lines.

Then she rushed in, slaying those demons that held his pride at bay. She forced her way through the front lines; giving way to her plight, and protecting his compassions.

Then she pushed aside the wreckage; shoving away the damaged pieces. She bid a good riddance to the unclean. She chased the evil from the recesses.

Then she stood up with a mighty battle shout, boastful in sound, and yelled to the world, "This war is over and it's a time for rest! Can't you see...he's had enough?!"

As the fog lifted and the enemy had decreased to zero, she helped him to his feet once again.

And then...can you guess what happened?

Then she whispered, "Now, I will fight for your heart, just the way you have fought for so many others."

Better-

Maybe it's just me, Just you. A different sight; A simpler view.

A newer sight, Opinionated fight. Hearts that won; Saw a new light.

A brand new world, An open book. An older life; A clearer look.

A gentle smile, A batting eye. Drifting clouds; A bluer sky.

Calmest of tides, Sunset rays. Happy minds; Better Days.

I Could-

I could plummet into your heart.
I could dive headfirst.
I would drown in your love.

I would die of thirst.

My lungs would be empty.
My heart could be restless.
They'd no longer function.
I'd remain still; breathless.

If love left me weak;
No longer able to heal,
It could leave such scars,
It would be so unreal.

But, in life, it's just not the case.
We sustain with every last breath.
I could live my days for you.
I could love you to death.

Short But Sweet-

I'm still a tiny-bit light headed when it comes to thinking of you at times.
I found myself a little free handed when it came to handing you a heart.
I constantly get somewhat dizzy when you spin the world off track.
I tend to lose a lot of time when by your side.
Sometimes I get speechless when it comes down to "I love you".

It takes me longer to write a piece of poetry these days. I guess it is due to trying to find a more creative way to write it most of the time. I do love poetry for being an energy within me. It's just another way I feel as if I am caring towards myself and towards others. I wouldn't trade it for the world.

Chapter Twenty-Six

We'll Burn That Bridge

When We Get There

As I was told as a child, "Don't go burning bridges...or be careful of the bridges you burn..." or something to that effect. Whatever that quote or variation of it was, it stuck. The quote that I like as an adult is,
"The hardest thing in life to learn is which *bridge* to cross and which to *burn.*" -David Russell

Now, we build bridges for trust, for friendship, for love, and sometimes the likelihood that two people have learned to interact on a common ground. Some of our bridges are built with very little material. (We figure that if we build a small one, it won't be so bad if we have to burn it someday?) Some of us also build massive bridges where it could be imagined to be aesthetically pleasing. I believe it is important that all these types of bridges to be constructed.

Life is about making connections; closing the gap. I love building these connections. I think it's a big part of empathy towards others. At times, I think I built too many, but they were built by me nonetheless. There have been plenty of people that I have had the pleasure of building these with. I have thought about this for awhile now. You never get to choose the material that you get to build with and it is never a one person job. Two people come together to build a relationship on a piece of ground of trust, friendship, and companionship.

Compassionate people are really good at building bridges. We are by far the greatest constructs of the unconscious. Our minds and hearts are forever strengthened. We build them quickly and we build them good enough to last. I know what you're thinking, "Man this book is chopped full of metaphors". It's all relatable in the end.

I think the problem with all these bridges, either made strong or weak, is they are destroyed just as easy or more easily than they are built. The visual of a burning bridge is also relatable. To burn is to destroy and to burn something means it either has to be rebuilt or you never get it back the same way ever again.

And on the other hand, compassionates are really good at leaving bridges standing for too long. Given the fact of my many bridges I have built over the years, I have not yet afforded myself the opportunity to burn as many as I should have. I guess it's playing a fool's game, just hoping to win. I imagine some of them have worn with the weather or suffered corrosion with rust, but they are still standing. God Bless us, the sentimental souls, thinking that time will change and maybe one day that bridge will be utilized once again. Wishful thinking is incorrigible. We are always going to hope for the best. You know, better days and all?

What we need to get better at doing is actually burning the bridges that we desperately need to burn. Burn them down without regret. What are we proving in keeping them? What are we trying to tell others by having them?

What I am saying is that in order to keep sane and ensure our own version of happiness, we have to let go. We have to be stubborn for this type of happiness. I have learned to rid myself of the unwanted. This is coming from a person that had a little different motto in years past.

I used to use my own version of the "bridge" saying, "Be careful of the bridges you burn, you might need to cross them again." and "Make sure when you burn your bridges that you have enough to rebuild them.". I used to think a lot of these bridges...these connections...they held more relevance in the scheme of things. I know I hated to see others leave my life. No matter what the consequences were, I always feared losing someone; a part of me. These were people I had placed in my heart with connections that were all built so long ago, yet sometimes my bridges were burned by others. In the wake of what burned, the remaining fires had to be put out by me.

What I guess I am trying to say is that there is so much time that is wasted when we are supposed to be living. Don't get me wrong, you should always build and find a way to communicate with other kindred souls, but try not to stay hopeful and helpless on a bridge while you're waiting to see if something/someone is going to come back.

Chapter Twenty-Seven

The Closer You Get

The Harder I Fall

Every morning, no matter how hard it is, I wake up, get out of bed, and realize that I was granted one more day. I think, "This little life of mine is truly a celebration." I don't know, most days it just puts a smile on my face. We all know life is rough but we are all here to live it the best we know how and Lord knows, we could be a lot worse off. Sometimes we cause many of our own afflictions without any help from others. Although, we find a lot of negative spaces here, we choose to smile. We choose to see another day; a better day. We choose these days of positive feelings, smiles, laughter, and love. Throughout all the negativity we endure, we will always find three things. Those are Love, Laughter, and above all, Compassion. Those three things will keep you moving, always.

We, as empathetic and compassionate people, have our drawbacks. We believe in more things than we care to. We care for a lot of people we haven't met or have ever known. We fall in love too quickly, too easily, and oftentimes too heavily. It's our character. Maybe it means that we were shown how to love others from a very young age. Maybe it somehow imprinted unto us. It is something that works, letting others know we care. Now, maybe it's considered a fault, we hurt ourselves time after time for the sake of it. We realize that it's a part of life that in order to stand, we must often fall.

I have a memory, like many other memories of when I was younger, that is very kindred. When I was in grade school I had a crush on this wonderful human being. She is still wonderful and still beautiful, inside and out. This was either third or fourth grade (the time I really started loving others) and she was a friend of mine. I was hopeful and hopeless. I bought her birthday presents, Christmas gifts and Easter gifts. I tried so hard to gain her favor. Cupid had made his shot and it hit me broadside. I want to say that she is the reason I started writing poetry.

She was adopted by her family and at times, I felt I could have been by mine. I felt I didn't fit in at times within my own family. It made sense that we kind of had that connection. I remember being an emotional mess over not being able to feel the love I thought I needed to receive from her. It was hard to be friends with the girl that liked every other guy but me. We were friends. We were friends that had the same friends, so we were hardly apart whether it was in class, recess, or even talking to each other on the phone. I suffered as much as I thought I could until I moved away in seventh grade. I had to leave everything I knew of school, life, and love. I left her behind.

Who's to know if anything would've changed if I was allowed to stay. Maybe her heart would've changed during the more important years after middle school. More often than not, life doesn't present itself like the plot of a movie's love story. It could've been wishful thinking. I never won her heart. I lost that battle. Far too often, I lost those battles in order to keep people in my life. I chose to lose far too many battles that ultimately I felt I could've won. Maybe if I could've stayed and fought it would've proven to be a win. Who knows.

She was the first realization that I could love outside my family. She was an awakening. I know, as a little boy as emotionally driven as I was, I drove her crazy just to get her to look at me differently. I smothered her without actually being a part of her world. Needless to say, I hated that word...smothered. I always thought that if you love something show it, but as I stated before, I tended to come on a little strongly most of the time. She taught me how to be a friend though and I love her for it. I couldn't thank her enough for that small, simple lesson.

Let's face it, sometimes love hurts. I mean, that's why people say it right? But as I see it, the most compassionate souls will tend to exude the greatest amount of love through the most damaged of hearts.

I am not saying that I didn't fall for many others (so many others). When they let me get close, I fell harder for them. It never got easier. It never hurt less than the times before. I continued to embellish my love for others for years. Love and compassion grew more and more beautiful to me. I loved the fact of loving others.

This is the mess I had made and honestly, I had issues with the clean-up for years. Would I trade it? No. Loving people and being compassionate to another person is a granted and reasonable mess I will take any day. The feeling I get when I get to share that mess I have made is the most wonderful part.

Chapter Twenty-Eight

Now Don't You Understand

That I'm Never Changing Who I Am

Every day, as I generally tend to do, I wake up early to make me a cup of coffee and get started with my day. I take time to scroll through the news or social feed and pretty much take time to connect to not only the world but back to myself. I don't really pay attention to the negativity of the media but look for the enlightenment others have shared. I typically listen to music. Music varies so much for me. I grew up with parents and friends that listened to incredible music. Now, I can't tell you who composed any arias and couldn't tell you anything interesting about an opera or oratorio, but I do appreciate it. I do listen to different music though. Most mornings my mood tends to be of an old rock or an alternative selection; sometimes old country. Music is definitely something that has kept me happy. You probably guessed that already judging by the titles of all these chapters.

Three great quotes:
"If music be the food of love, play on." -William Shakespeare

"Music, at its essence, is what gives us memories. And the longer a song has existed in our lives, the more memories we have of it." -Stevie Wonder

" Listen to your inner-voice: Surround yourself with loving, nurturing people. Fall in love with your art and find yourself. Music is the great communicator." -Glenn Hughes

I like to think that a lot of great compassionate people share this trait with me. I believe all my friends and family relate to music in this way. It connects us.

I sit and think of all the similarities that people like me share and even if they do not share all these wonderful things with me, at least we have a bond somewhere in the scheme of things.

I love to think they all compassionate people think the same way; with the same heartfelt connection as I have with the world. It's truly not as optimal as I picture it but I like to think it is close. I wonder if they are animal lovers, write books or always wanted to write but couldn't form the words, or have a voice that can embody the greatest of singers. Maybe we have all come from a heartache that we survived and this is how we deal with the world by loving each other. Yet, maybe we all have known sadness and all we want is to share a little laughter with others. Are these the lives we love to lead?

I have come to the path of my life where I want positivity; I want life to be laughter. I am not a perfect person nor do I ever claim to be and I still believe that depression never quite leaves you. I do believe that music, laughter, and love for another human being or animal is key to being happy.

I was negative for so many years of my life. I hated a lot of things. I played the victim when I could. I was emotionally stir-crazy for a good bit. But now...I want so much more and being disgruntled about life is no way to get it.

So here I am. I am trying.

I can't seem to imagine a life that I am without the feelings I have. Some days, I can be an over-emphatic, sobbing wreck due to an ad on t.v. or a story I read on Facebook, but I am not changing it. I'd rather stay drunk with love than be rich because of hate. This is my great escape finally free enough to tell people I love them and that I appreciate them. I don't care nor give a damn if they don't share it with me. The good thing about love and understanding is that it doesn't always have to be both ways. I am sure to tell all the ones I love that I do so because at least they know. It's good to be held to that standard. A great compliment to life is to be loved. I think so anyway.

Chapter Twenty-Nine

The Hook Brings You Back...

On That You Can Rely

I have generally taken a path to better understand others. Sometimes those paths proved to be harder on me than I anticipated. I like learning things from experience. Lord knows, I don't study things or research as much as I should. Generally, I take experiences and relate them to actions. I believe it connects me to people. People relate to experiences and what they felt when it happened.

I am stubborn in the way of remaining to be compassionate to each and every person I meet. This shouldn't come as any real surprise. I just live to experience things time after time and learn from them.

I have always said that I wanted to express an uneducated view on what I have chosen to experience and then share my thoughts on it. I also believe that we mostly learn far more from actual experiences than trying to interpret what others have written.

The problem is that there is a really fine line between a friendship and a relationship. It's true that it can change at any moment. We are just waiting for these miraculous moments to happen. We wait for these life changing enigmas that we ourselves are yet to figure out and then they become frustrations.

So, let's talk about the subjects of "Friend Zones" and the fact that nice guys finish last. We can all agree that these are two of life's little issues; frustrating enigmas as I have stated.

Needless to say, I'm a Libra. I know that tends to explain a lot to a great number of people that know the characteristics of the astrological signs. Libras are the lovers. Every Libra you'll ever meet is the same. We care too much and get hurt easily. Some don't like to admit it and rarely show it, but we have a habit of dying on the inside. Trust me, I know. I haven't been able to change it. It's just a part of me.

I hate the Friend Zone! I hate it for other people. It'll drive you to drink. We are told so many things throughout our lives. They are not necessarily untrue but maybe a little unbelievable. I was told all my life that love is easy when friendship is already there. This is not true all the time. Friendship, mind you, does help but it is just one lonely key amongst a slew of others waiting to open but one holy door. I would say I owned a plot of land in the very inhabited city of Friend Zone. A land that I never profited from. Nothing ever grew there even though it was nurtured for years. It was never considered a dessert but it was never an oasis either.

I never considered myself to most attractive of guys but damn I had heart. If you ever heard of a guy that was fearful of what others thought, I was one of trepidation. But, I had friends. I had friends I loved (secretly loved). I was guilty of listening to their horror-filled dating experiences, their tales of sorrow, and their questions about the whereabouts of the guy that would treat them right. Meanwhile, I very calmly set off a bomb in the back of my mind while screaming, "Damnit, he's here! Why are you not seeing me!?"

This zone, where it is common place to throw your doubts and insecurities as far as friendships, is a glitch of human behavior. I know that the discussion of this could go on forever, questions of who puts who there more often, but it tends to happen to us guys...a lot. I spent many years there; being compassionate to an end. That's how it goes sometimes, being compassionate until it ends. I learned a lot of lessons from the Friend Zone. Throughout all the talks of how shitty the other guy was or how imperfect she thought she was, I did pay attention. You know how to get out of the Friend Zone? You leave. You make your feelings known. I don't know about you but when it came to having friends, I had plenty. If someone can't understand the feelings you have, then that is their problem. I think the moral is: Don't spend years loving someone more than a friend when they can't spare a few minutes to love you.

I know that what I am saying kind of sounds indifferent and I am not saying lose your friendships over the reality of a made up but all too real place, but instead, communicate. Ask the questions that you need to. Ask if you are better off friends or is it worth the loss. Talk it out or try it out. Who's to say that it'll work out or not? At least, you both will know how each other feels and then you'll be free to make a decision.

I am happily married now and my wife is the greatest of friends. But, once upon a time, I took the chance to tell her that I wanted to be more than friends.

With that being said I also want to share this. The greatest people, the greatest ideas, and the greatest beliefs often end up at rest and go unheard. They died far too soon. They are always mentioned as a whisper when they should've had an echo. Far greater things have gone unmentioned, denying our spirits a more memorable standing.

Now, on to the subject of finishing last.

I never wanted to compete with others and therefore finishing last wouldn't have been anything relevant to me. Somehow, when you're in a competition with someone, it seems to matter a little bit more. I had my own demons to contend with much less trying to keep up with others. Sometimes, the competition finds you, tries to beat you, and leaves you dead last. It leaves you defeated and it leaves your ego deflated.

Competition seemed to be a likelihood in everything I did. I never wanted to finish last. Hell, I just wanted to be a part of the race. That is satisfying enough. Just to get one shot; do or die. I have spent my life giving second, third, and even fourth chances. Those chances gave me the title of being a compassionate and a forgiving person. I gave more chances than I ever should have but I gave them without hesitation, never allowing myself to see a bad outcome. In a moment of hope, I tended to hope for a chance to be given back to me.

Nice guys finish last...
 It's been that way since the inclusion of time itself. It seems like a balance. It's a balance of good and bad where the nice guys sit and patiently wait, often in the Friend Zone, just to see if there's a slight chance of coming in first. It seems we need this balance.

 Throughout all the years of missed opportunities, bad timing, and getting my hopes up, I still respect this odd balance. Sure, I certainly would've had a better chance of taking risks when I was younger if I would have realized this balance. I stayed in the Friend Zone and continued to finish last because it put me in a place I felt wanted at the time. If I didn't have the trials and errors of this world then I wouldn't have had been placed into this incredible life that has made me who I am and more of who I want to be. I never wanted to break the mold but instead I wanted to make the mold.

 Compassion makes us strong. Always remember that. It costs nothing to have it. It has made great things. I have made great friendships and, with those wonderful friendships, I have created a circle of heartfelt people that I would never trade for anything.
 If I have to deal with these realities that only affect me as a compassionate soul yet make me stronger, then bring it on. I will continue to finish last and be a friend just to save another.

Chapter Thirty

I Never Dreamed I'd

Love Somebody Like You

I was born with a hole in my heart. I am only speaking figuratively but it's so relatable right now. The idea of a hole in this heart is precious to my thought process. I think that if I have a place to put anything for safe keeping, a hole is just as good as any. I have put many things there...Love, friendships, religion, feelings I love to share with others, and memories that will forever fortified by my belief that there is always a better day. I was born with a hole in my heart I am glad that I have found so much to fill it with. I chose to fill it with beautiful imperfections that I have found perfect.

Long before I gained this new understanding of how I was meant to be, I had to come to a realization. Everyone that ever told me that before I could truly love anyone else I had to love myself was completely right. Every flaw I ever saw in myself I had to either accept that I couldn't change it or learn to love a little imperfection. The view of perfection isn't honest. Perfection will lie straight to your face and make you lust for something you have been told was right.

When I hit a growth spurt in my teenage years, I lost a lot of weight. This is the crazy part. That little chubby kid still inhabited my self esteem. I was a little chubbier than that of my younger brother as a child, so some chubby little boy jokes were said. I tried not to appear too affected by them as I was in my teenage years the after-effects of the jokes seemed to linger. I hid a lot of things emotionally and being chubby kind of hit a nerve. As I have stated before, I was an emotionally driven kid. I stayed skinny throughout my high school years and even skinnier when I joined the service. I did look odd being that thin. I didn't bulk up again until I married a woman that cooked. I have been big ever since. By far, I am the heftiest of all my family. I realize that I need to exercise and take better care of myself but I am more comfortable in my skin these days. I'm not saying that I don't look into a mirror at times and think, "Shit, exercise...eat more fruit!"

Mirrors show us some ugly truths that we do not want to see sometimes. My mirror shows me the signs of me getting older. I hate that. I feel young. I want to still look young. Don't we all? Yeah, I notice the gray hairs that I know I have had since I was twenty-two and the dry (yet oily) combination of my skin. It seems every time I have to shave, my face seems to look more weathered; more tired. Harrison Ford said it best as Indiana Jones when he quoted, "It's not the years honey. It's the mileage." Would I trade it? No. Would I ever have surgery to correct it? Again, no. I have accepted that what I see in the mirror isn't what others see. Other people truthfully see the things you choose to not see yourself. There are some beautiful people out there that aren't perfect. I am not perfect for myself but when it comes to being perfect for others, well...that's not my decision is it?

A particular song came to mind and was almost the title of this chapter. It's one that I have listened to for years. My dad listened to older music all my life. Being somewhat of an old soul, I love the classics. One of the first Eagles' songs I ever heard along with "Hotel California" (also a great damn song) was "Learn to Be Still".

I once thought it was a primarily religious song with the lyrics stating such things as "We are like sheep without a shepherd", " and wind up following the wrong gods home", and "and one more starry-eyed messiah'. But I , along with others, have thought a little differently over the years. It's more of a "Love Yourself" song.

I think in plain language it is about us always thinking that there is something brighter on the other side. I believe it's about people who believe that because either the relationship they're in, their friendships, the place in which they live, their choice of job, or something else entirely is something they aren't completely satisfied with. There's always going to be something or someone that's unsatisfying in all these aspects. When you're old enough to actually look in the mirror and just be honest with yourself, you start to discover that much of the problem is you. That is why everything such as the new job, relationship, life, or location never ever seems to solve the problem. This is where my vision of a mirror comes to play. I believe this song is more about looking in a mirror, simply changing yourself and your thought process and attitudes towards life, counting your blessings and really being thankful for what you have. It's about learning to be still.

It's hard not to notice if you look hard enough and find an understanding of why things are the way they are. Loving yourself isn't without purpose. You do it in order to survive. Loving others is the easiest thing in life to do. That's why it hurts so bad when it's over. Something so simple and so easy is always thought to be painless. But look at the heart of the matter,...you have sustained hurt many times before and yet you have survived simply by choosing love. Always learn to be still and to love you for you, the others will follow.

Better Days was a book that was a journal turned into something I was truly proud of and always will be. It is a book of heart that came from me. It dealt with my life, my depression, and a love I didn't quite understand but saw that things could get better. It took fifteen years to write. This one took a little less. The purpose of both Better Days books is to share and to encourage others. Although, I do tell a lot of my personal feelings within both, I choose to write from the heart; a message of hope. It connects us. I wouldn't want it any other way.

Sometimes, things in our lives; they fall apart, they come together, and may or may not be always within our control. There's one of two things to do and that is either become a part of the tragedy or simply sell tickets to the show; this awesome show we call "Life".

Always keep yourself moving. Move forward, move away, move towards, or move despite what others say. Move forward so that you aren't pushed back. Life is about movement and it is ever changing. As they say, "If you aren't moving forward; you're standing still." A former boss once told me, "Always move towards things. Always keep moving towards something. You are never getting anything by standing in one place. Before too long, standing still gets you buried; probably by someone who is moving".

No matter what, always try to be compassionate first. You never know what people have been through. There is always someone worse off than you. There is always going to be someone that better than you. But, I tell you this, compassion is going to win out every time. So, be sure to tell the ones you care that they are loved, that they are a part of your world, no matter how great or small. Far too often we lose touch with people; with hearts. I have lost too many people in my life that I never got to say how much I cared for them. Whether it is just moving away from others or losing them in death, it's always hard to say goodbye. Make someone feel beautiful or memorable whenever you can. Always let them know.

So, to one compassionate heart to another, try to stayed connected...always.

Thanks for the Memories

One of the most wonderful things about Kerry is that he is a wonderful friend. He is someone I admire as well as love. I have many wonderful memories with him and I know I will have a lifetime more. He gives anyone and everyone a beautiful gift that's worth more than all the money in the world. It is laughter and a smile. I hope he never changes. God blessed me by sending Kerry into my life. I can't count the many times I needed his shoulder to cry on. Thank you so much. You are the best Kerry Jeffrey. Love Ya!

- Kendra Hall (Brooks)

When I was in 8th grade, I moved back to Texas from Missouri and Kerry was one of the first to befriend me. It was harder for me to make friends. I was not what you would call a popular kid. I was not from a wealthy family although wealth is so much more than money and I was a newcomer. I was the kind of kid that joked around and cut up to get attention. I always tried to "fit" in with people but I didn't need to with Kerry. In 8th grade Kerry was a very funny, talented, caring and giving person that would always be there as a friend and that continued into high school. Kerry invited me over to his house on several occasions although looking back I might have kind of invited myself. Kerry was a really good friend to me throughout school and is still a good friend today although we have not seen each other in years. I am privileged to say that he is one of my friends and I will never forget how much his friendship helped me in life. Friends are one of the most important things a person can have and this is my way of saying thank you Kerry for being one of mine.

- Duane Gross

When you're in high school, you think you will never grow up. When you grow up, you think you were never in high school. It's kind of crazy to look back at all of the years and realize you really didn't walk away with much. I mean who really cares if you made a rough draft before your final copy or how you got to the answer to the algebra problem? The things I took with me into adulthood were great people. People I love like family. I have a close knit of people that I spent most of my school days with and we get together when we can to enjoy memories and our families. One of those friends is Kerry.

I don't have the best memory so I can't say for sure when we first met. I think it was around seventh grade. It's the most awkward age for any child. Junior high was when you started to find yourself, and maybe lost a little of yourself too. I remember Kerry and I rode the same bus to and from school. He was this tall, skinny kid with a bush of white blond hair and a laugh that either made you join in or drove you crazy. I happen to love laughing, so I always joined in!! We were compatible friends from the beginning and since I am not really shy, I got all the information in the first bus ride. I knew then that he was someone who would imprint on my life and make me a better person for knowing him.

Kerry was what you would call the class clown. He always had a witty quip for any conversation and a comeback for any remark. He still does. You can't be mad around Kerry or sad for very long. He won't allow it. He is the glue that keeps us connected and we love him all the more for it. This book took a lot out of Kerry but he has given so much to us. I cannot imagine a world without you my friend. I hope we still get together in the next thirty years and we can toast to your success at life. I am thankful to call you a friend.

- Stacie Walker (Owens)

When I was in the 9th grade, I had world geography class with Kerry. I always looked forward to this class due to the fact that it didn't matter how my day was going, I knew it was about to get better. For Kerry always had a way to make me laugh and turn my day around. Kerry would tell jokes and sometimes use silly voices to make me laugh. Kerry was part of the group I hung out with, in some ways he was best of us. He was the guy you could tell your secrets too and you knew, even if he didn't agree with you he would still stick by you. He has helped me in many ways; he has been a shoulder to cry on, someone to cheer me up, and a caring and honest friend. I still enjoy listening to his jokes and hearing about his two beautiful kids. I admire his ability to be honest and his ability to draw and laugh at just about anything. In many ways I am a better person because he is my friend.

-Tammy Wheat

There are few people you meet in high school you want to forget and some you can't forget. When I met Kerry, I thought he was one of the sweetest guys I'd ever met. He always knew what to say to me if I was upset and did a great job. He always drew pictures for me (which I loved). One year he got me a little stuffed bunny for Easter. No one had ever gone to the trouble like he did to make me smile. I always wondered why he never asked me out. If he had of.... I would have said yes. Like I said before, there's some you want to forget but Kerry is one who you will cherish forever. A great friend and a great person! Here's to long lasting friendships.

- Rachel Dunklin

On my eighteenth birthday, I received a present from Kerry. It was a big teddy bear I lovely named Jeffrey. I named him after Kerry, kind of. Jeffrey became my best friend substitute as I went through college, as I started my adult life, and when I could not see my friend. Jeffrey has since been passed on to my children and still continues to wear our senior shirt. I'm not sure how it happened but somehow the connection between Jeffrey, Kerry, and I is so strong. It seems like every time there's a crisis in my life, Kerry instinctively knows that my heart strings are pulling at his and he seems to call at the perfect time. The line that runs between my heart and Kerry's has no call waiting, dropped calls, busy signals, and it always has service. I couldn't imagine not having Kerry in my life and I love him so much.

- Claudia Wyatt

Wow!! Kerry wrote a book! Very interesting and intriguing! I always saw Kerry walking down the halls at school, and it was always like a ray of sunshine. Never ever did I see him without a smile on his face. Kerry dated one of my best friends in high school so I was always on the outside looking in. When I was around Kerry my cheeks hurt from smiling and laughing the entire time. When I would look at Kerry I would think his life must be perfect because if it wasn't then how could he be so full of happiness all the time. I also know how Kerry treated his girlfriend and he treated her like a princess. She was the center of his world.

Kerry was an awesome boyfriend which was something that I wanted badly just by watching him with her. Anyway, needless to say after 10+ years since I have seen Kerry, my memories of him are of that smiling face, his contagious laughter, the joy that seemed to follow him everywhere, and the joy and happiness that he brought to everyone who encountered him. Congratulations to Kerry and his amazing adventure that this book has been for him as well as others.

- Melissa Long

We met in the spring of 1998 when I was forced by my mother to spend my spring break visiting family. Although we are related, we had never met each other before this time due to living in different states. Upon arriving at our Aunt Evelyn's house, I was surrounded by a ton of people that I did not know and had probably met at some point in my life but did not remember. In the midst of all these people stood a person that seemed kind of like me even though different states and a few years age difference separated us. Both of us were shy but when you get to know us we never shut up, and both with biting sarcasm. This person was you. Even though we did not spend a lot of time together that day, I kind of felt like I had finally met someone in my family that made sense to me and that I felt I could mesh with.

Although there were a few years that we lost contact, when we finally found each other again it was as if that time had never passed. I finally found someone that I can talk to about anything with, and I do mean ANYTHING. Whether it's listening to me complain about stuff going on in life or just to listen to the utmost random stuff that pops out of my head, I don't quite know if you realize how much you mean to me. I always say that you are like the brother I never had (although you're my cousin), but you are actually more than that to me and words can never truly express how much I appreciate you (even though I never say it.) I just hope that you realize that I will always be here for you at any time of day and anywhere life takes us both.

I never really understood or tried to fit in with my family and since meeting you, I see that while family is important, it is also important to create your own niche instead of trying to fit yourself into a mold that you would never go into. Although sometimes you drive me absolutely insane (when you wake me up with random things) I'm sure the feeling is mutual. Just remember that although I may be a deer widow every October, you have traveled to places in Arkansas I've never seen. I love you and wish only the best things for you in life and know that anything you put your mind to will be achieved. Don't let people get you down, and when they do, just remember that I will always be here to help you pick back up the pieces. I love ya!

-Jessica Hardin (Lowe)

Anyone that knows me knows that I surround my life with kindness and love. Family and friends are first and foremost. I have never put myself first when it comes to the love I give them. My greatest friends, it seems, have been around for it seems like forever. I love them as family and sometimes I treat them better than myself. I am blessed with a lot of sisters and a couple of brothers. I wouldn't trade them for the world.

A big thank you goes out to all of you. You know who you are. I never thought I'd love this big group of people as much as I do. Thank you for being there for me and I am forever thankful for you. This book was written for you. So that you can be a part of my life as much as you've been a part of mine.

www.ingramcontent.com/pod-product-compliance
Lightning Source LLC
LaVergne TN
LVHW081346060426
835508LV00017B/1434